がⓇできるだけではなく、ひとりの天才を軽く超えていくような、創造的な解を得る可能性も開かれる。しかし建築が今、民主主義と大衆主義のあいだで揺れているように、世論や市場の暴力に抗い、より創造的で、普遍的な解を導くことができるのかどうかは、建築にとって大きく、また困難な問いであり続けている。

設計とは本質的に孤独である、ひとりで考えればよいのだと開き直ることも可能であろう。でも私たち建築家はいま、AI（人工知能）の技術が進化し、より多くのデータを直接扱うことができるようになった社会で、多様性を認め、寛容な社会の実現を信じて、より多くの知恵が集まれば集まるほどよりよいものができる、と言い切ることに挑戦するべきではないだろうか。

本書では建築を知識と形態の創造的な関係＝「ちのかたち」としてとらえ、設計作業のあらゆる断面を建築的思考のプロトタイプとして等価に扱うことを試みる。設計の履歴を可視化することで、その時どきでの判断を積み重ねるだけでなく、あるプロジェクトで学んだことを次のプロジェクトに応用するというように、生み出す建築をより深く、新しいものへと進化させることができるだろう。そしてその作業をより多くの人で行い、ときに機械による計算を伴うことで、建築的な思考のパタンを組み合わせ、より多くの人でよりよいものを生み出すことを目指す、集合的な知をかたちづくる方法論へと展開し、建築を社会のさまざまな課題解決に向けた、創造的な知のツールとして再定義したい。

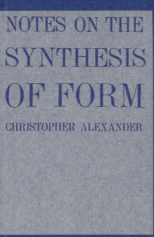

● Christopher Alexander, *Notes on the Synthesis of Form*, Harvard University Press., 1964

● クリストファー・アレグザンダー著 『形の合成に関するノート』、ハーバード大学出版局、1964

conduct research of the surrounding area and refer to history; another effective way would be to return to the basic approach of collecting more knowledge — because "two heads are better than one", as the saying goes.

It is possible to find more reliable solutions — or even more creative solutions that would go way beyond ideas of a lone genius — by collecting sufficient amount of opinions, even if some of them may seem banal. Under the current situation where architecture vacillates between democracy and populism, it remains a great and difficult challenge for architecture to find creative and universal solutions while withstanding the severity of public opinions and impacts of fluctuating markets.

One may defiantly declare that architectural design is fundamentally a solitary act to be carried out by a sole individual. However, we architects should acknowledge diversity, convince ourselves that we can realize a more tolerant society and declare that we can achieve better results by collecting more knowledge in today's society where we can directly handle a much larger amount of data using highly advanced AI technology.

In this book, architecture is understood as a "form of knowledge" or a creative relationship between knowledge and form, and any segment of design processes is treated equally as a prototype of architectural thinking. By visualizing records of design processes, we are able not only to keep up our efforts of ad hoc decision making but also apply what we learned in one project to the next one. Architecture we create will further evolve into something new through such efforts. We intend to develop a methodology formulating collective knowledge that aims to combine patterns of architectural thinking and produce better results through involvement of more people and occasionally incorporating computer-driven calculations in the making process and redefine architecture as a creative tool to create knowledge for solving various social issues.

The Form of Knowledge

The Forn
edge —
type of A
al Thinki
Applicat
Fujimura

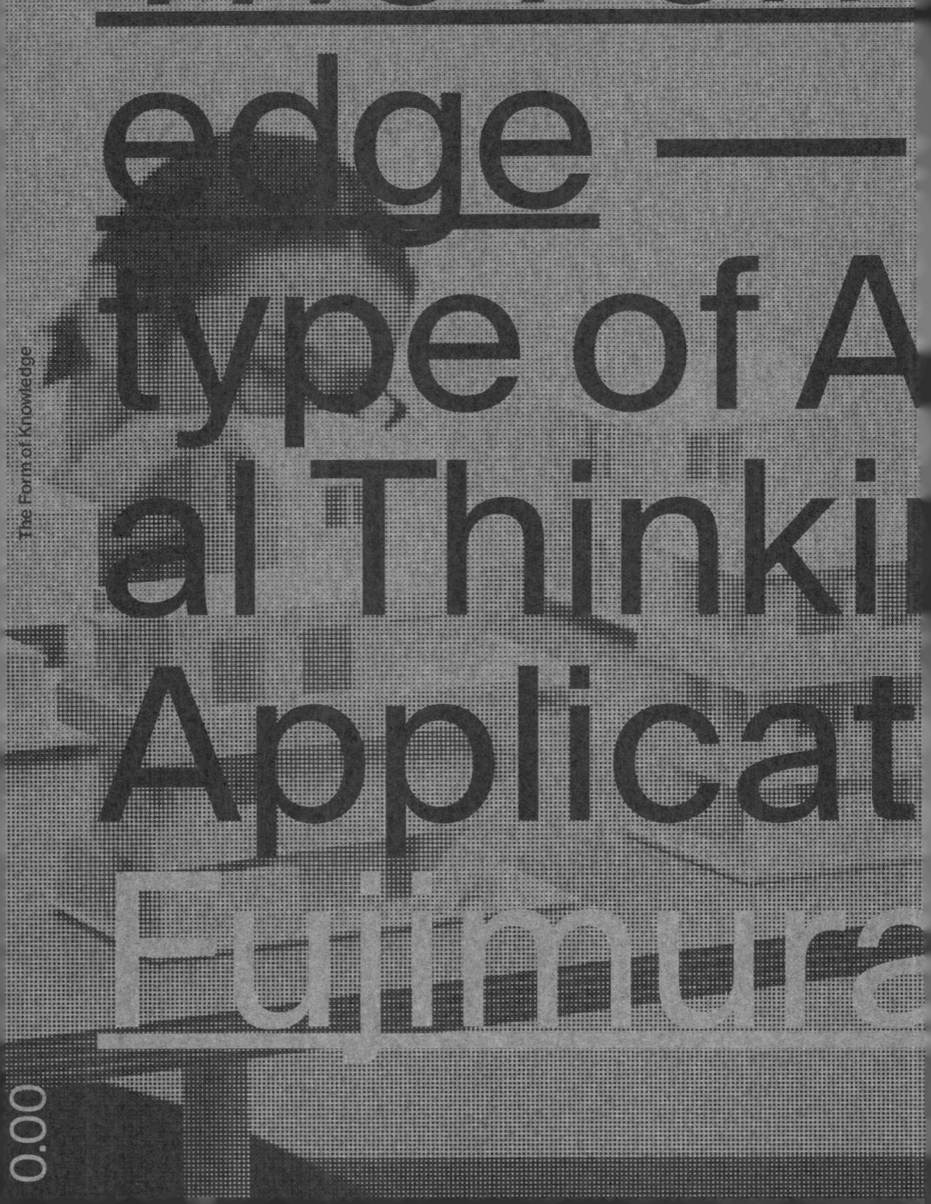

of Knowl

The Proto-

chitectur-

g and Its

on – Ryuji

007

ちのかた

000

008

The Form of Knowledge:

The
Knowl
edge —
type of A
al Think
Applicat
Fujimura

0.00

009

g200r05

of Knowl
he Proto
chitectur
g and Its
on — Ryuji

0.00

Contents

0.00	001	The Form of Knowledge	
0.0	016	Visiting Fukushima and Drawing a Line	
0.1	016	**Visiting Fukushima and Drawing a Line**	2011–
0.2	032	**Axis of Question**	2012
0.3	034	**Odaka Pioneer Village**	2018
0.4	050	**Timeline – as a Method of Approaching the Difficult Whole**	
1.0	054	Super Linear Design Process	
1.1	056	**SHOP U**	2005
1.2	072	**BUILDING K**	2008
2.0	096	Semiotic Experiments: X HOUSE	
2.1	098	**Building HOUSE**	2009
2.2	112	**Storage HOUSE**	2011
2.3	132	**Shed HOUSE**	2011
2.4	146	**House HOUSE**	2012
3.0	168	Mass Learning, Mass Decision	
3.1	170	**Tsurugashima Project**	2011-16
3.2	182	**Facility for Ecology Education**	2014
4.0	206	Give form to Collective Knowledge	
4.1	208	**Aichi Project**	2013
4.2	224	**G Chair**	2014
4.3	234	**G House**	2014
4.4	242	**Shiraoka Newtown Project**	2016
5.0	262	From Semiotic to Continuous: Three Experiments with Apartment Building	
5.1	264	**APARTMENT S**	2011
5.2	276	**APARTMENT B**	2013
5.3	288	**APARTMENT N**	2014

目次

0.00	001	ちのかたち	

0.0	016	フクシマへ通い、線を引く	
0.1	016	**フクシマへ通い、線を引く**	2011–
0.2	032	**問いの軸**	2012
0.3	034	**小高パイオニアビレッジ**	2018
0.4	050	**タイムライン──複雑な全体(difficult whole)に近づく方法としての**	

1.0	054	超線形プロセス	
1.1	056	**SHOP U**	2005
1.2	072	**BUILDING K**	2008

2.0	096	記号をめぐる試行錯誤──○○の家	
2.1	098	**ビルの家**	2009
2.2	112	**倉庫の家**	2011
2.3	132	**小屋の家**	2011
2.4	146	**家の家**	2012

3.0	168	集団で学ぶこと、集団で決めること	
3.1	170	**鶴ヶ島プロジェクト**	2011-16
3.2	182	**鶴ヶ島太陽光発電所環境教育施設**	2014

4.0	206	集合的な知にかたちを与える	
4.1	208	**あいちプロジェクト**	2013
4.2	224	**G Chair**	2014
4.3	234	**G House**	2014
4.4	242	**白岡ニュータウンプロジェクト**	2016

5.0	262	記号から連続へ── 3つのアパートの試行錯誤	
5.1	264	**APARTMENT S**	2011
5.2	276	**APARTMENT B**	2013
5.3	288	**APARTMENT N**	2014

Contents

6.0 308 Towards Collective and Continuous Architecture

| 6.1 | 310 | **OM TERRACE** | **2017** |
| 6.2 | 334 | **Tsurugashima Central Community Center** | **2018** |

7.0 356 Architecture as A Form of Knowledge

7.1	358	**Subaru Nursery School**	**2018**
7.2	392	**Deep Learning Chair**	**2018**
7.3	408	**Architecture as A Form of Knowledge**	**2018**
7.4	416	**Axis of Hope**	**2012**

8.0 418 **Articles | Yoshikazu Nango**

Drawing a Line -
Architectural Thinking of Ryuji Fujimura

9.0 429 **Study of "Discrete Space"** 2018

10.0 444 Postscript

11.0 450 Data

11.1	452	**Data on Works**
11.2	456	**Profile / Staff List**
11.3	457	**Credits**
11.4	458	**Data of Books**

目次

6.0	308	集合的かつ連続的な建築へ	
6.1	310	**OM TERRACE**	2017
6.2	334	**つるがしま中央交流センター**	2018

7.0	356	「ちのかたち」としての建築	
7.1	358	**すばる保育園**	2018
7.2	392	**Deep Learning Chair**	2018
7.3	408	**「ちのかたち」としての建築**	2018
7.4	416	**希望の軸**	2012

8.0	418	**寄稿文｜南後由和**	
		線を引くこと——藤村龍至の建築的思考	

9.0	429	**「離散空間」のスタディ**	2018

10.0	444	あとがき

11.0	450	データ	
11.1	452	**作品データ**	
11.2	456	**略歴/スタッフリスト**	
11.3	457	**クレジット**	
11.4	458	**奥付**	

018 | 0.0 | Visiting Fukushima and Drawing a Line

0.0 フクシマへ通い、線を引く

020

0.1

Visiting Fukushima and Drawing a Line

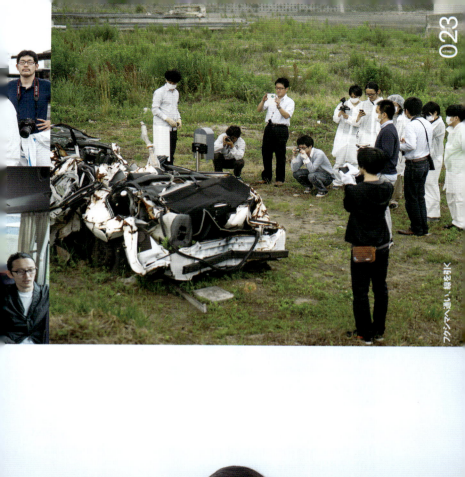

フクシマへ遣い、線を引く

0.1

0.1 | Visiting Fukushima and Drawing a Line

One day in March 2011, immediately after the Great East Japan Earthquake, critic Hiroki Azuma called me up and asked me to present a recovery plan of a disaster-struck area in the critical magazine *Shisou Chizu beta* directed by Azuma himself. As a first step, Azuma gave me a ride to see the disaster-struck areas in Tohoku. On the way home, he asked, "Would you like to think about Fukushima?" and told me that the problems in Fukushima would be especially worth challenging to think compared with problems in other areas including Iwate and Miyagi which can be mostly solved only through construction work. It was exactly the kind of theme-setting one would expect from a thinker.

It was indeed a difficult task. I had expected tasks in which architects are able to make the best use of their expertise, including planning of facilities such as a community assembly hall or temporary housing, which involves communication with parties concerned, or larger-scale tasks of removing "misfits" between infrastructure and its context, such as designing of seawalls that residents feel an affinity with and planning a housing layout that harmonizes with nature for a relocation project of a seaside community to a higher ground. Architects would be able to communicate their ideas using visual images in such cases and I had imagined that these are the kinds of proposals where architects can fully utilize their expertise.

I clearly remember the moment when Toyo Ito said, "I am sorry to say that there is nothing architects can do for Fukushima" at a symposium I attended at the University of Tokyo on November 2, 2011. First of all, construction of nuclear power plants in Japan, including the one in Fukushima, was decided and implemented during the post-World War II modernization period. Nuclear technology was supported and developed by the Japanese industries and became an indispensable technological infrastructure in our daily life. Moreover, it has become one of Japan's major exports. Due to the gigantic scale of the nuclear system, it is beyond architects' abilities to envision how the system can be changed.

0.1 | フクシマへ通い、線を引く

2011年3月某日、東日本大震災の直後、批評家の東 浩紀さんから連絡があり、東さんが主宰する批評誌『思想地図 beta』(コンテクチュアズ)で復興計画を提示してほしいと依頼された。まずは被災地を見に行こうということで被災地へ向かう東さんの車に乗った。帰り道、「福島について考えよう」と言われた。岩手や宮城の復興計画は建設工事でなんとでもなるが、原発被災地である福島の問題は考えるに値するという。なんとも批評家らしい課題設定だった。

難しい宿題をもらってしまった。建築家が得意なのは例えばコミュニティのための集会施設をつくる、仮設住宅の配置を考える、などコミュニケーションに関わるものか、防潮堤を親しみのもてるものにする、高台移転を自然になじむものにするなど、ラージスケールの工事とコンテクストとのミスフィットを取り除くか、どちらかではないかと思っていた。それらは絵にしやすいし、建築家らしい提案になりやすい。

2011年11月2日、東京大学で行われた「シンポジウム：311ゼロ地点から考える」(TOTOギャラリー・間 主催)で「残念ですが、福島に対して建築家ができることは何もありません」と伊東豊雄さんがおっしゃったことはよく覚えている。原子力発電所の事故は何よりも戦後の近代化のなかで意思決定がなされ、日本の産業界が技術を育み生活を支える技術の一部となり、さらには日本の貴重な輸出品の一部ともなっている。あまりにも大きなシステムであるから、その変更は建築家が提案できる領域を超えている。

そんなときこそ、課題を具体的にとらえるという建築家の十八番を生かさない手はない。私の最初のアイデアは、それまで住んでいた土地に住めなくなった住人たちがコミュニティを維持するために集団移転しかないだろうということであった。かつて奈良県十津川町の住人たちはかつて大規模な水害に遭い、北海道に集団移転をして「新十津川村」をつくったし、アメリカ軍に占領された沖縄の住民は石垣島に計画移民を余儀なくされた。

ちょうどその頃、福島第一原子力発電所のある双葉町の行政機能が埼玉県のさいたまスーパーアリーナに移転していた。埼玉県は東日本大震災のあと死亡者数がゼロで災害が少ない場所だったこともあり、福島県から埼玉県にたくさ

Architects should make the best of their ability to understand specifics of existing issues at a time like this. My initial idea was to relocate the entire group of people who were forced to move out of their homeland to another place and sustain their community there. In the past, residents in Totsukawa Village in Nara Prefecture lost their land to a major flood and relocated to Hokkaido to restart "Shin Totsuka -mura" (New Totsuka-mura) on a new land. After the United States military started the occupation of Okinawa, some of the local residents were forced to systematically relocate to Ishigaki Island.

Around this time, the municipal office of Futaba-town (the town where the Fukushima Daiichi Nuclear Power Plant is located) relocated to the Saitama Arena Stadium in Saitama Prefecture. After the Great East Japan Earthquake occurred, many people evacuated to Saitama Prefecture from Fukushima Prefecture, because Saitama Prefecture was barely damaged by the disaster and had no casualties. Under such circumstances, we presented a proposal envisioning the establishment of Little Fukushima in Saitama Prefecture.

I made numerous visits to Fukushima. During the visits, I toured inside the evacuation area with disaster victims and asked them how it was before the disaster. Sometimes I went inside the nuclear power plant in protective clothing and interviewed people working there. I saw a gigantic cantilevered structure used for decommissioning work, as well as many workers who were sent to the site to engage in decontamination work which was implemented at an enormous cost.

I kept thinking what kind of architecture Fukushima needs and what I should do to precisely understand issues in Fukushima from an architectural point of view. Eventually, I found that the axis line running from Fukushima to Saitama extends beyond and passes through Hamamatsu and Okinawa. I conceived an idea of calling it "Axis of Question" and decided to find an answer to the question. Architecture is not just about drawing lines to solve a problem. In my view, drawing a line to pose a question is also part of architecture.

んの人が避難していた。そんな埼玉に「リトル・フクシマ」をつくってはどうかという提案をした。

福島へは何度も通った。被災者の方たちとともに避難区域のなかを回り、そこがどんな場所だったかを聞いた。ときには防護服を着て原子力発電所のなかにも立ち入り、東京電力の社員からも話を聞いた。廃炉作業に用いられる巨大なキャンチレバーの構築物や、湯水のごとくコストが費やされる除染作業にたくさんの人が動員されていた。

福島に必要な建築は何か、福島を建築的にとらえるにはどうすればいいかを考え続けた。やがて福島から埼玉へと向かう軸線は浜松と沖縄を通ることがわかった。戦後の国土形成の過程で課題となった原発・郊外・移民・基地と代表的な課題が入っていることに気がついた。私はこの軸線を「問いの軸」と呼ぶことにし、その答えを探すことにした。解決のための線を引くだけが建築ではない。問いのための線を引くこともまた建築である。

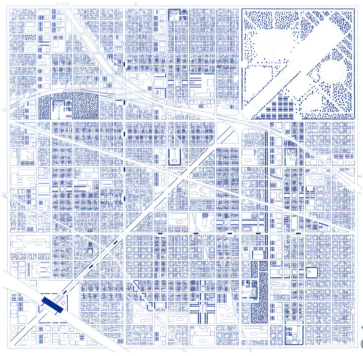

● Ed. Hiroki Azuma, *shisouchizu beta* vol.2 (2011)
● 東浩紀 編著『思想地図 beta vol.2』(2011)

● Little Fukushima (2011)
●「リトル・フクシマ」(2011)

029

フクシマへ通い、線を引く

0.1

032 | 0.2 | Axis of Question

Axis of Question

OKINAWA d

0.2

035

時田皮膚科医院

小高パイオニアビレッジ

0.3

0.3 | Odaka Pioneer Village
is a small-scale multifunctional facility for generating new jobs in the area devastated by the nuclear power plant disaster.

During my frequent visits to Fukushima, I became acquainted with a group of young local people based in Minamisoma who engaged in disaster recovery activities. I noticed that they had expanded their business on a larger scale than before the earthquake by making the best use of human network they had developed through disaster recovery activities. Before long, they asked me to design a small building used as a new activity hub for disaster recovery. My initial thought was that our design should communicate their vitality to overcome the devastating nuclear accident in a physical form.

The young Kenzo Tange [1913-2005] proclaimed that he intended to "build a factory of peace" when designing the Hiroshima Peace Memorial Museum [1955]. Although "a factory of peace" might have been too grand an expression for the required function of the memorial museum, I sympathize with his idea of envisaging the exhibition facility as a factory to recreate daily life in Hiroshima, the city devastated by the atomic bomb.

The small hub for disaster recovery requested by the client was a facility comprising a maker's space, co-working office and guesthouse. I expected that this hub would potentially become a "factory of new daily life" in the disaster-struck area. Generally speaking, factories are often closed off to outside to protect confidential information, but in recent years there is a new trend to actively open up factories to outside in order to show manufacturing processes and also to incorporate social contribution activities.

Our design started from setting a large centripetal space in anticipation of hosting events, but we gradually came to realize that it would make more sense to place the required

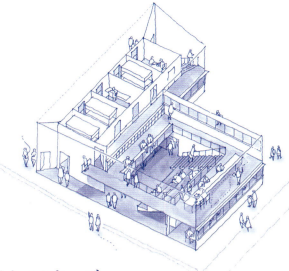

0.3 小高パイオニアビレッジ
は、原発被災地に新しい仕事を生むための
小規模多機能施設である。

福島の原発被災地へ通ううちに、南相馬を拠点に活動する若い地元の人びとと出会った。被災後、被災地の復興支援に集まった多彩な人材のネットワークを生かし、気がつけば震災前より事業を拡大させ、新しい事業を生み出していた。やがて彼らから新しい復興の拠点をつくりたいからそのための小さな建築を設計してほしい、と依頼を受けた。原発事故による強烈な被災経験を乗り越える彼らのバイタリティをかたちにしたいと考えた。

若き日の丹下健三[1913-2005]は広島平和記念資料館[1955]の設計に際して「平和の工場」をつくると宣言した。求められた「資料館」という機能に対して「平和の工場」とはなんとも大げさな気もするが、求められた機能は単なる展示施設でも、目指すべき機能は広島の原子爆弾被災地に日常を再生産するための施設=工場であるという丹下の考えには共感できる。

復興のための小さな建築に求められたのはメイカーズスペース、コワーキングオフィス、ゲストハウスを含む施設で、それはいわば、福島の原子力発電所事故被災地に新たな日常を再生産する「工場」であった。一般的に工場といえば企業

functions such as to "work", "stay" and "create" in sequence of a single flow of time. While one of the ways of spreading information about their activities would be to organize events, I felt that we could also reach out to people in a subtler way: we can take visitors on a tour inside the building and show them how new "daily life" is recreated here.

We focused on designing a "small flow of time" by creating a continuous circulation inside the building. Visitors are first lead into a stair-like space in the office. After attending a lecture there, they take a tour through the atelier and guesthouse and arrive at the shared office in the end.

"The new base for disaster recovery activities" is a "job factory" or a facility to create jobs to sustain new life in disaster-struck areas. It is important to promote their activities by "building a job factory", and it was necessary

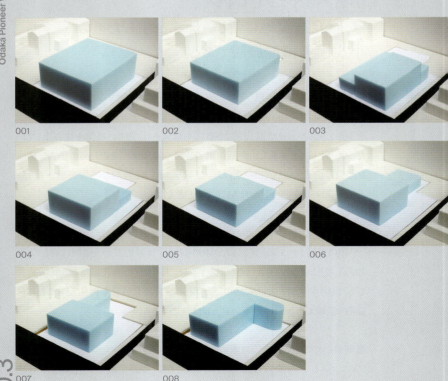

001   002   003
004   005   006
007   008

の機密を保持するために外部に対して固く閉ざされる場合が多いが、近年ではものづくりのプロセスを発信する装置としてむしろ積極的に外に開く場合も多い。

当初はイベントの開催なども想定して、大きく求心的な空間を想定した。だがやがて理解できたのは、求められた「仕事をする」「宿泊する」「ものをつくる」などの機能を、ひとつの時間の流れのなかに置くことが、よりふさわしいということだった。イベントの開催による外部への発信の仕方もあるだろうが、ここでどのように新しい日常が再生産されるのか、視察に訪れた人びとに建物のなかを案内するような、静かな発信の仕方もあると感じられた。

そこでオフィスには大きな階段状のスペースをつくり、そこでレクチャーを受けた人びとはアトリエを見学し、その後ゲストハウスをめぐり、最後にシェアオフィスにたどり着くひとつながりの動線をつくり「小さな時間の流れ」を設計することが大事だと考えた。

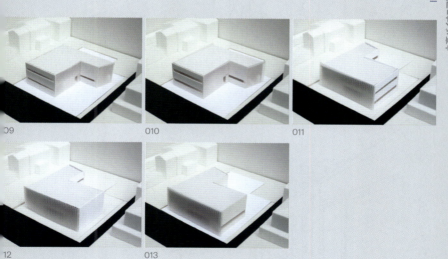

to design a "small flow of time" to take a tour around the "job factory." The question of "how we should design the job factory" finally emerged when an answer to the initial question of "how we should transform required functions of 'work', 'stay', and 'create' into physical forms" gradually became clear.

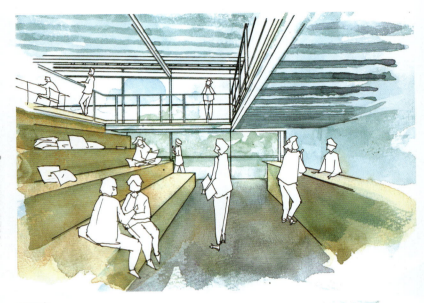

「新しい復興の拠点」とは、被災地の新しい日常を支える仕事を生み出す装置＝「しごとの工場」であり、「しごとの工場をつくる」ことを通じて復興の様子を発信するためには「しごとの工場」を見学するための「小さな時間の流れ」をつくることが重要であると気がついた。「しごとの工場をどうつくるか」という大きな問いは、「仕事をする」「宿泊する」「ものをつくる」という、「新しい復興の拠点」のためにとりあえず想定された機能をかたちにする過程で、「小さな時間の流れ」をつくるという答えが見えてきた頃に、ようやく浮かび上がってきた。

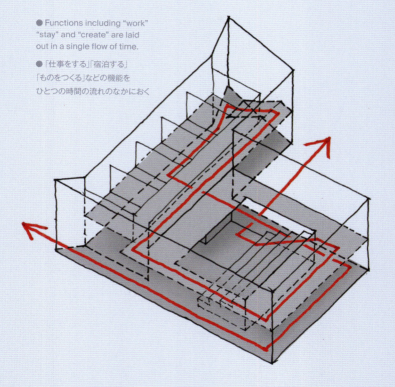

● Functions including "work" "stay" and "create" are laid out in a single flow of time.

●「仕事をする」「宿泊する」「ものをつくる」などの機能をひとつの時間の流れのなかにおく

● It is a plain box like a factory. Walls are translucent and activities inside are projected through them and visible from outside at night.
Above: Hall
Below: Maker's space

● 工場のようなそっけない箱。ただし壁は半透明とし、夜はなかの様子が外に映し出される。
上：ホール
下：メイカーズスペース

#	English	#	日本語
1	Hall	1	ホール
2	Maker's space	2	メイカーズスペース
3	Kitchen	3	キッチン
4	Office	4	事務室
5	Washroom	5	洗面所
6	Dressing room	6	脱衣所
7	Bathroom	7	浴室
8	Toilet	8	トイレ
9	Under-stair cupboard	9	階段下収納
10	Staircase	10	階段室
11	Equipment space	11	設備スペース

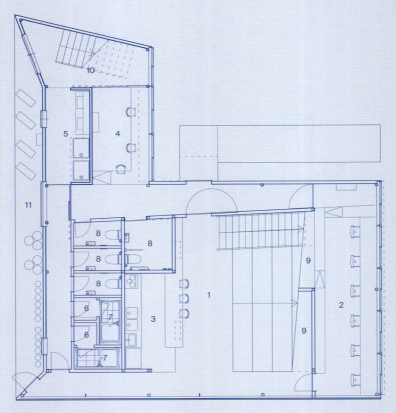

1F plan | 1F 平面図 | 1:150

1	Co-working space	1	コワーキングスペース
2	Guesthouse	2	ゲストハウス
3	Corridor	3	廊下

● Floor plans with slightly angled walls. Excessive dimensions are eliminated. Subtle movements create a rhythm in the sequence.

● 壁に少しずつ角度がついた平面。無駄な寸法を削り落とし、わずかな挙動がシークエンスにリズムを与える

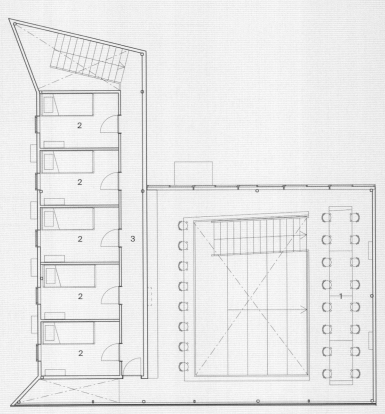

2F plan | 2F 平面図 | 1:150

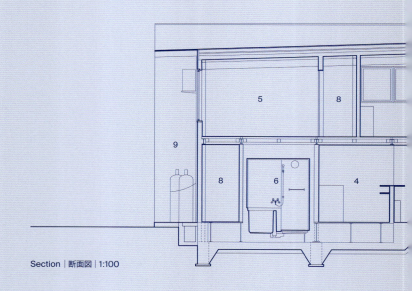

Section │ 断面図 │ 1:100

1	Hall	1	ホール
2	Maker's space	2	メイカーズスペース
3	Co-working space	3	コワーキングスペース
4	Kitchen	4	キッチン
5	Guesthouse	5	ゲストハウス
6	Bathroom	6	浴室
7	Under-stair cupboard	7	階段下収納
8	Corridor	8	廊下
9	Equipment Space	9	設備スペース

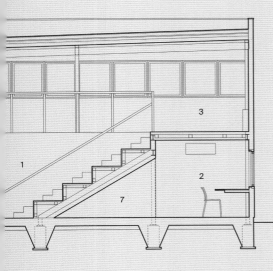

● Section with large symbolic stairs in the center. A maker's space, co-working space, kitchen and guesthouse are placed three-dimensionally around the stairs.

● 象徴的な大きな階段を中心にした断面。メイカーズスペース、コワーキングスペース、キッチン、ゲストハウスが階段のまわりに立体的に配置される

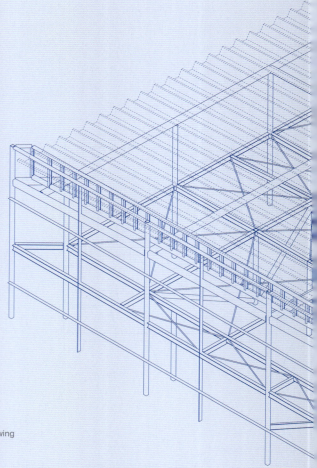

- Structural axonometric drawing
- 構造アクソノメトリック図

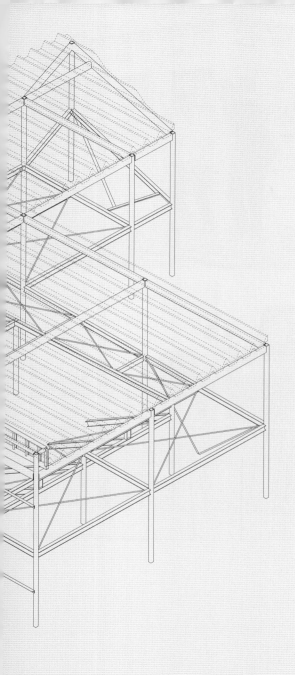

小商いパイオニアビレッジ

List of components | 部材リスト

Pillars | 柱
□-100×100×6
■-100×100
H-148×100×6×9

Beams | 梁
H-148×100×6×9
□-100×200×9
H-150×75×5×7

Braces | ブレース
H-148×100×6×9
M30
□-100×100×3.2
〇-76.3×3.2
M16
M20

小高パイオニアヴィレッジ

0.4 | Timeline — as a Method of Approaching the Difficult Whole

Architects currently face complex questions of how architecture should involve itself in post-disaster efforts for the Great East Japan Earthquake. Among the disaster issues, the Fukushima Daiichi Nuclear Power Plant accident poses the most complicated and challenging question of how architecture should deal with the nuclear accident. It is extremely difficult to grasp the issue in its entirety.

In Complexity and Contradiction in Architecture, Robert Venturi suggested that simplification through reduction should be avoided and the "difficult whole" through inclusion should.

Be achieved instead it still remains a big challenge for architects in the post-Venturi era regarding how we can avoid monotony that Modernism fell into, understand the difficult reality we face and create a new difficult reality through architectural design.

When the internet became publicly available in the 1990's, the entire system was called a "cyber space" and its concept was understood by using an analogy with "real" spaces, as exemplified by terms such as the "home" page or virtual "mall." Since the 2000's, on the other hand, people began

0.4 | タイムライン──複雑な全体（difficult whole）に近づく方法としての

東日本大震災と建築がどう関わるかは、建築家にとって複雑な課題である。まして福島第一原子力発電所の事故と建築がどう関わるかは、全体像のみえない、実に複雑な課題である。

かつてロバート・ベンチューリは『建築の多様性と対立性』（原著 1966 ｜ 伊藤公文訳、鹿島出版会、1982）のなかで排除による単純化を避け、包合による「複雑な全体（difficult whole）」を獲得することを呼びかけた。ベンチューリ以降の建築家にとって、近代主義が陥った単調さを回避するために、建築の設計を通じて複雑な現実を理解し、再び複雑な新しい現実を設計することそのものは、大きな問いであり続けている。

インターネットの世界では、1990年代にそのシステムが普及した頃、その全体はサイバー「スペース」と呼ばれ、「ホーム」ページだとか仮想「モール」だとか、現実の空間に置き換えて理解されようとしていた。だが2000年代以後のSNSでは、TwitterにせよFacebookにせよInstagramにせよ、インターネットの全体を時間の流れ＝タイムラインで理解するようになった。ならば建築が直面する社会の「複雑な全体」もまた、その広がり＝スペースに着目することよりも、流れ＝タイムラインに着目することで理解され得るのではないか。

もともと政治の世界には「漸進主義（インクリメンタリズム）」という、政局の局面ごとに最適な判断を繰り返して少しずつ理想に近づいていくという考え方がある。ソフトウェア設計の世界では、プログラマたちが設計を行う際に、すべての要件を定義して設計を行う「ウォーターフォール」に対して、決まったところから順番に固め

to understand the entire Internet world as a flow of time or "timeline", as seen in social networking services (SNS) including Twitter, Facebook and Instagram. Given this circumstance, the "difficult whole" of society that architecture faces today may be understood by focusing on its flow or "timeline" rather than its extent or "space."

—

Incrementalism in politics is a model of policy making process by repeating decision making processes to reach the best results through incremental changes. In software design, "Agile" software development is a flexible and incremental method of finalizing each part where decisions have been made one by one, as opposed to the "Waterfall" model software development, which is a method of defining all requirements before starting design.

—

One of the lessons I learned through my frequent visits to Fukushima is that a more effective approach in responding to the serious disaster recovery issue in Fukushima would be to outline project requirements first; start working from what we already know and transform our ideas into forms one by one; and gradually clarify questions and answers through the course of time, rather than to clarify the entire issue first before starting design.

—

If the work involves a procedure of roughly sketching out an overall picture based on "what to do" in one's mind first before incorporating them in design drawings, it is a space-based approach. On the contrary, if one makes efforts to incrementally articulate "what to do" based on things that have been decided without sketching out an overall picture, it is a time-based approach. In that case, the question and answer regarding "what should be built" would be often articulated at the very last stage of the design process.

—

Architects generally excel at space-based thinking. This is exactly why they tend to think too spatially and simplify things when addressing an issue. Another strength of architects is the ability to transform each finding into a form part by part, gain new finding and gradually articulate the whole by repeating the process — which I call a timeline-based thinking.

ていくことで成果を出そうとする「アジャイル」という考え方が対比されている。

福島に通う日々のなかで私が学んだことのひとつは、「福島はいかに復興するべきか」という大きな課題に応えるためには、その問いの全体像を最初に明らかにしてから設計に取り組むよりも、まずプロジェクトを設定し、わかっていることから順番にかたちにし、時間の流れのなかで徐々に問いと答えを同時に明らかにしていくことが有効であるということだ。

最初に「するべきこと(what to do)」のかたちを大まかに頭に描いてから設計図に落とすという作業がもしあるなら、それは実に空間的なアプローチである。対して全体のかたちを頭に描くことをせず、決まったところからかたちにすることで「するべきこと(what to do)」に漸進的に近づく作業があるとすれば、それはとても時間的なアプローチであるといえるだろう。その場合、「何をつくるべきか(what do we built)」という問いと、それに対する答えは、往々にして設計が終わる頃にようやく描かれることになる。

建築家は空間的な思考に強い。だからこそ建築家は課題に取り組む際に、空間的に想像しすぎて、単純化してしまうことがある。建築家のもうひとつの強さは、時間の流れのなかで、わかったことをひとつずつかたちに置き換え、そこからまた新たにわかったことをかたちに置き換え徐々にその全体像を定めていく、そのタイムライン的な思考ではないだろうか。

1.0 | Super Linear Design Process

054

Super Linear Design Process

General Design Process
一般的なプロセス

Super-Linear Design Process
超線形的なプロセス

1.0

| 1.0 | 超線形プロセス

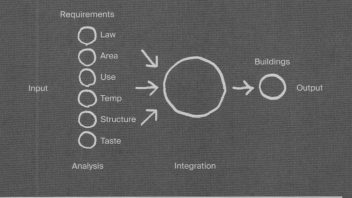

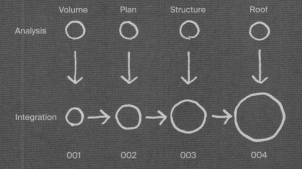

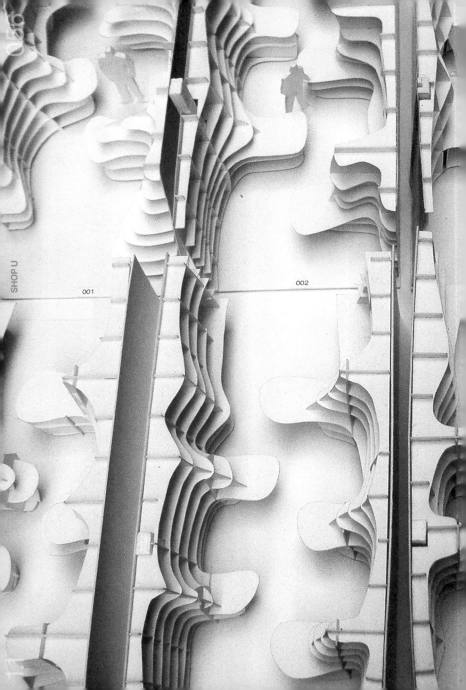

SHOP U
is an interior of a tableware store.

The process of pursuing an unknown goal is more enjoyable than planning backward from a predetermined answer. There is nothing more boring for architects than participating in a project with a predetermined set of "what to do", such as simply meeting all floor area requirements. What we architects propose at the planning stage would be more important than what we present at the design stage.

When the client commissioned us to design her first tableware store, she didn't have a clear overall picture for what she wanted. Our first scheme had the simplest volume possible, surrounded by 30cm-deep display shelves all around.

After seeing our model, the client told us that although she liked the uninterrupted view inside the space, she was concerned that it was too open and customers might hesitate to enter. In response to her comment, we made a model composed of several divided spaces and presented it to her. But her reaction was that the space was divided up too much and it would be difficult to talk with customers. She also wanted to maintain some distance between the store staff and customers to encourage a smooth conversation. In response to her remarks, we made a model composed of "bumps" projecting from the right and left sides and presented it to her. This time she liked the scheme, and we enjoyed these gradual design development through quick exchanges of ideas between us and the client.

In product design, the process of quickly making a model based on a new idea is called "prototyping." By quickly repeating the process of prototyping, presenting a model and getting feedbacks from the client, we come up with a form we had never seen before.

1.1 | SHOP U
は、食器を扱うショップのインテリアである。

正解に向かって逆算するのではなく、決められていないゴールに向かって探求する過程は楽しいものである。建築家にとって、与えられた面積表をただクリアするように、「するべきこと(what to do)」の定められたプロジェクトに参加させられるほどつまらないものはない。私たちの仕事はデザインのレベルの前に、プランニングのレベルで何を提案するかが重要である。

テーブルウェアのショップを開こうとするクライアントは、当初自らの最初のショップについて具体的なイメージをもっていなかった。私はまずできるだけ単純なヴォリュームを想定した。棚はせいぜい30cmほどの奥行きだろうからそれをぐるっと一周させただけのかたちであった。

クライアントに見せてみると、見渡せるのはいいが、見渡せすぎて入りづらいのではないかと言われた。ならばと思い、空間をいくつかに分ける模型を見せた。すると、空間が分かれすぎて入ってきた人に自然に声を掛けられない、もっと自然な距離をつくりたいと言われた。ならばと左右から突起を出した模型を作って見せたら、いいんじゃない、と言われた。この短いやり取りでちょっとずつ前に進む感じが楽しかった。

プロダクトデザインの領域で思いついたアイデアをかたちにすることを「プロトタイピング」という。軽くプロトタイピングしてクライアントに見せ、反応を見てまた次の模型をつくる。どんどんバージョンをつくっていったら最後に見たことのないかたちが現れた。

060

SHOP U

001
002 
003 
004 
005 
006 
007 
008 
009 
010 
011 
012 

1.1

013

014

015

016

017

018

019

020

021

022

023

061

SHOP U

1.1

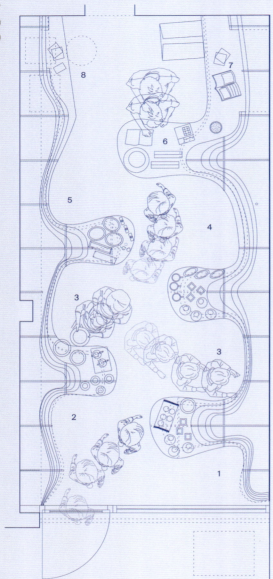

1	Display corner
2	Discount tableware
3	Western tableware
4	Japanese tableware
5	Luxury tableware
6	Counter
7	Gift wrapping counter
8	Office

1	ディスプレイコーナー
2	特価品コーナー
3	洋食器コーナー
4	和食器コーナー
5	高級品コーナー
6	カウンター
7	包装台
8	事務コーナー

● Winding circulation creates a space where customers are invited to linger around unconsciously, while indicating different merchandize sections including western, Japanese, luxury, and discount tablewares.

● 蛇行する動線は洋食器、和食器、高級品、特価品と異なるジャンルの食器のまとまりをつくりつつ、客が自然と長居することも可能な空間をつくり出す

Plan｜平面図｜1:50

The bumps projecting from the right and left sides configure the space into four zones with the store staff's zone in the back. The four zones are used to display products from respective categories including discounted products, Japanese tableware, Western tableware, and luxury products. The meandering circulation naturally invite customers to stay longer.

Generally, it is considered that design requirements should be predetermined before the design process starts. When starting a new project, however, one needs to start a design process by conducting research to determine design requirements. As we devoted ourselves to the design process prompted by vigorous exchanges with the client, we realized that we were conducting research to determine design requirements and developing design at the same time, which felt like a journey without a destination. It was indeed a refreshing and enjoyable experience.

左右から突起の出た棚で4つの領域をつくり、一番奥に店員の領域がある。この4つの領域は特価品、和食器、洋食器、高級品とジャンルごとに並べることができる。蛇行する動線は訪れた人が自然と長居することを可能にする。

—

これらの要件は、本来であれば設計を開始する前に定義されていなければいけないものである。だが新しいプロジェクトの場合、デザインの作業は要件についてリサーチし、定義することから始めなければならない。クライアントとのやり取りに夢中になってデザインを進めていくうちに、その作業は要件のリサーチとデザインが平行しており、どこにたどり着くかわからない経験であることに気がついた。それはとても清々しく、楽しい経験だった。

● The shopfront. The organic form allures passersby to enter.

● 店の構え。有機的な形態が外の客に呼びかける

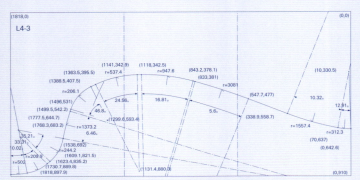

Detailed shop drawing 1 | 加工詳細図1 | 1:200

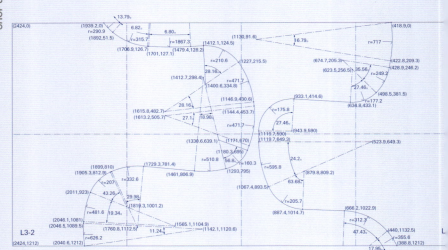

Detailed shop drawing 2 | 加工詳細図2 | 1:200

● In 2004, design and manufacturing operations were not connected yet. Curves were machine-cut at the factory, and craftsmen did the rest of the work including processing and assembling.

● 2004年の時点では、まだ設計と施工は連動しておらず、カーブだけを工場の機械でカットし、そのほかは職人の手により加工され、組み立てられた

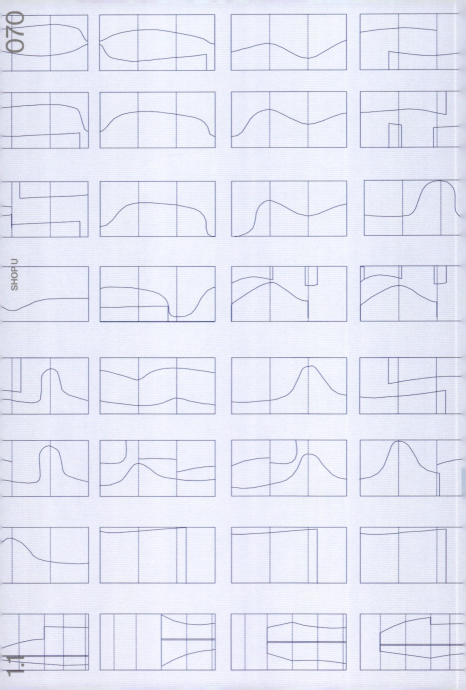

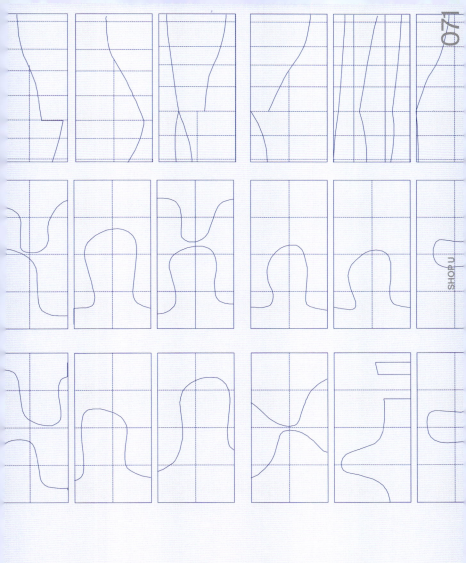

Wood cutting diagram | 板取図 | 1:600

073

BUILDING K

1.2

1.2 BUILDING K
is a mixed use building comprising apartments and a shop located along a shopping street in Tokyo.

—

When we laid out all the study models for "Shop U" in chronological order to evaluate the entire design process, I found that they all followed the same principle of "no jumping, no branching out, no going back." The entire sequence of these models displayed a continuous "timeline" illustrating an evolution of a building from a simple volume to a complex one. It was as if watching the incubation process from an egg to a fish.

The new project was at a much larger scale than the shop interior design we had done. My curiosity and willingness to free my mind and design from scratch were stronger than my ambition to realize the vision I already had in my head.

—

We started from placing a simple volume. Then we observed the model closely to determine which part to modify, and modified it accordingly. By quickly repeating the process, a new form comprising several "pencil buildings" standing atop a glass-clad transparent podium eventually took shape. A series of work sessions with a structural engineer and a building services engineer gave meaning to forms emerging from the process one after another: the gaps between the "pencil buildings" became a machine yard, structural cores, and natural ventilation pathways.

—

We had thirty-eight models at the end of the process, and found that twenty-one conditions were set during the model making process. We decided to call the time period between the moment when requirements were confirmed and the moment when design parameters were determined the "search stage", and the time period between the moment when design parameters were determined and the moment when the final form was determined the "comparison stage".

—

| 1.2 | BUILDING K
は、東京都内の商店街に計画された
集合住宅と店舗からなるビルである。

—

「Shop U」の設計にあたって自らのつくってきた模型を時系列に並べ、全体を振り返ったとき、それらが「ジャンプしない、枝分かれしない、後戻りしない」という原則に貫かれていることに気がついた。そのようにして作成された模型群は、ひとつの単純なヴォリュームが複雑なヴォリュームに至るひとつながりのタイムラインを示し、まるで卵から魚へと至る、生物の孵化過程を見ているかのようだった。

—

新しいプロジェクトはショップのインテリアよりはるかに大きな規模であった。できるだけ心を開放して、ゼロから建築を設計するとどうなるだろうという気持ちが、頭のなかに思い浮かぶ情景を実現してやろうという気持ちを上回った。

—

単純なかたちを置く。決められるところから決める。やがて透明なガラスの基壇の上にペンシル・ビル（細長いビル）が並んでいるようなかたちが生まれてきた。

Some tendencies were observed. For instance, the twenty-one conditions were determined by firstly setting large-scale conditions and eventually breaking them down into small-scale conditions. If small-scale conditions had been set in the beginning, possibilities for further design development would have been limited.

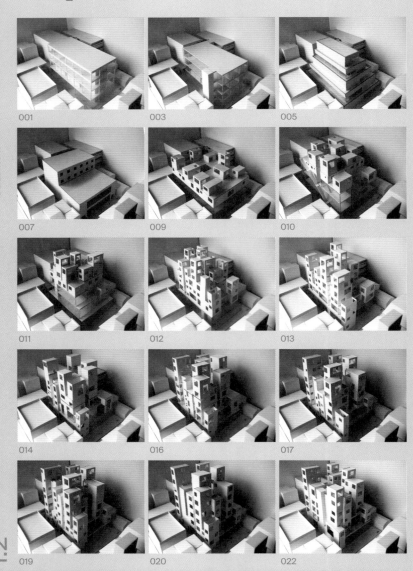

構造と設備のエンジニアとのセッションから、生まれていくかたちに次々と意味が与えられていった。
—
最終的に38個の模型が残った。それらを生み出すプロセスを振り返ると、21項目の条件が設定されてきたことがわかった。要件の定義が固まり、設計のた

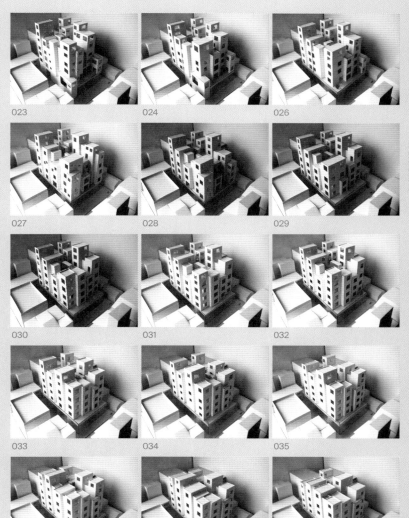

I decided to call this design pattern, which is implemented by repeating the process of transforming what has been decided into a form, finding an issue and a solution based on the principle of "no jumping, no branching out, no going back", the "Super Linear Design Process." It is not simply linear, but not so extraordinary as to be called "non-linear." We discover more creative solutions by articulating each step and repeating the process of integrating small emerging systems. This process may be associated with the experience of climbing a high mountain — we have already climbed up so high by the time we realize how far away the starting point appears in the distance.

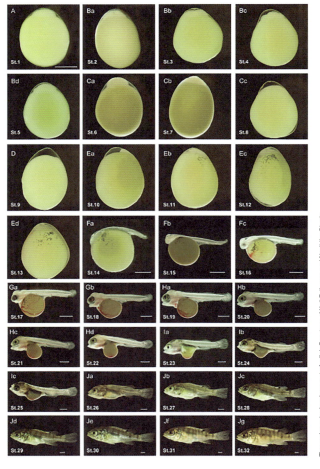

The embryonic development of a fish Courtesy of Koji Fujimura and Norihiko Okada, "Development of the embryo, larva and early juvenile of Nile tilapia Oreochromis niloticus (Pisces: Cichlidae); Developmental staging system," Development, Growth and Differentiation Volume 49 Issue 4, May 2007, Japanese Society of Developmental Biologists

めのパラメータ（媒介変数）が定まるまでのあいだを「検索過程」、設計が定まってから異なるケースごとに形態を比較して最終形を定めるまでのあいだを「比較過程」と呼ぶことにした。

—

いくつかの傾向があった。例えば21項目の条件は、最初は大きな条件から定め、小さな条件へと向かっていく。小さな条件を先に決めてしまうと可能性が狭くなる。

—

私は「ジャンプしない、枝分かれしない、後戻りしない」を原則として、とりあえず決まっていることをかたちにして、課題をみつけ解決するという単純なフィードバックを細かく反復するそのデザイン・パターンを「超線形デザインプロセス」と呼ぶことにした。単純な線形でもなく、非線形というほどマジカルでもない。手続きを都度明らかにして、生まれてくる小さなシステム同士の統合を繰り返していくと創発が起こりやすくなる。いつのまにか出発点が遠く感じられるほどに、高くまで登っているようなイメージである。

形態の境界条件項目／案no.	1	2	3	4	5	6	7	8	9	10	11	12	13	14	15	16	17	18	19	20	21	22	23	24	25	26	27	28	29	30	31	32	33	34	35	36	37	38	39	40
1 容積	●	●	●	●	●	●	●	●	●	●	●	●	●	●	●	●	●	●	●	●	●	●	●	●	●	●	●	●	●	●	●	●	●	●	●	●	●	●	●	●
2 構造（S造）			●	●	●	●	●	●	●	●	●	●	●	●	●	●	●	●	●	●	●	●	●	●	●	●	●	●	●	●	●	●	●	●	●	●	●	●	●	●
3 資料単位の違い（1階を最大）					●	●	●	●	●	●	●	●	●	●	●	●	●	●	●	●	●	●	●	●	●	●	●	●	●	●	●	●	●	●	●	●	●	●	●	●
4 用途（2階以上も共同住宅）						●	●	●	●	●	●	●	●	●	●	●	●	●	●	●	●	●	●	●	●	●	●	●	●	●	●	●	●	●	●	●	●	●	●	●
5 分散したヴォリューム									●	●	●	●	●	●	●	●	●	●	●	●	●	●	●	●	●	●	●	●	●	●	●	●	●	●	●	●	●	●	●	●
6 壁面分節（隣地のスケール）										●	●	●	●	●	●	●	●	●	●	●	●	●	●	●	●	●	●	●	●	●	●	●	●	●	●	●	●	●	●	●
7 垂直性の強調												●	●	●	●	●	●	●	●	●	●	●	●	●	●	●	●	●	●	●	●	●	●	●	●	●	●	●	●	●
8 内部プランニング（法規）															●	●	●	●	●	●	●	●	●	●	●	●	●	●	●	●	●	●	●	●	●	●	●	●	●	●
9 角のラインを通す																●	●	●	●	●	●	●	●	●	●	●	●	●	●	●	●	●	●	●	●	●	●	●	●	●
10 設備シャフト															●	●	●	●	●	●	●	●	●	●	●	●	●	●	●	●	●	●	●	●	●	●	●	●	●	●
11 立面縦スリット（排気口）																			●	●	●	●	●	●	●	●	●	●	●	●	●	●	●	●	●	●	●	●	●	●
12 サッシの規格																				●	●	●	●	●	●	●	●	●	●	●	●	●	●	●	●	●	●	●	●	●
13 吊構造																						●	●	●	●	●	●	●	●	●	●	●	●	●	●	●	●	●	●	●
14 開口のプロポーション																						●	●	●	●	●	●	●	●	●	●	●	●	●	●	●	●	●	●	●
15 基壇																									●	●	●	●	●	●	●	●	●	●	●	●	●	●	●	●
16 EV位置（最外周から控える）																									●	●	●	●	●	●	●	●	●	●	●	●	●	●	●	●
17 アスロックのモジュール																											●	●	●	●	●	●	●	●	●	●	●	●	●	●
18 開口のゆらぎをなくす																												●	●	●	●	●	●	●	●	●	●	●	●	●
19 一つのヴォリュームに一列の開口																												●	●	●	●	●	●	●	●	●	●	●	●	●
20 6階（近隣対策）																																		●	●	●	●	●	●	●
21 階段位置（ヴォリュームの隙間）																																					●	●	●	●

● The horizontal axis represents generations of models and the vertical axis represents rules found along the process.

● 横軸に模型の世代、縦軸に発見されたルール

● The hatching process from an egg to a fish. Starting from a simple volume, it is gradually articulated and becomes a complex whole.

● 魚の発生過程。単純なヴォリュームからスタートし、少しずつかたちが見出され、複雑な全体に至る

● A view of the construction site. The fifth floor is constructed of a mega-floor structural system supporting the upper volume consisting of the fifth and sixth floors and suspending the lower volume consisting of the second, third, and fourth floors.

● 建設中の風景。5階の床をメガフロアとし、2、3、4階を吊り下げ、5、6階は独立したヴォリュームとする

1	Shop	1	店舗
2	Common space	2	共用部
3	Equipment space	3	設備スペース
4	Bicycle parking	4	駐輪場

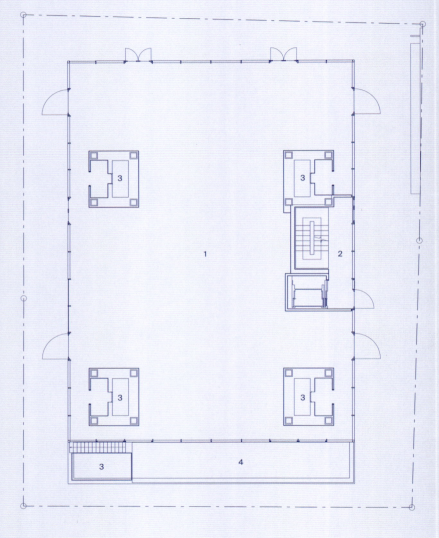

1F plan | 1F 平面図 | 1:200

1	Room	1	室
2	Common corridor	2	共用廊下
3	Equipment space	3	設備スペース

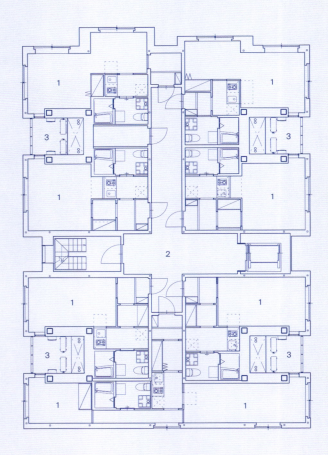

3F plan ｜ 3F 平面図 ｜ 1:200

BUILDING K

086

1	Room	1	室
2	Elevated walkway	2	空中路地
3	Equipment space	3	設備スペース

BUILDING K

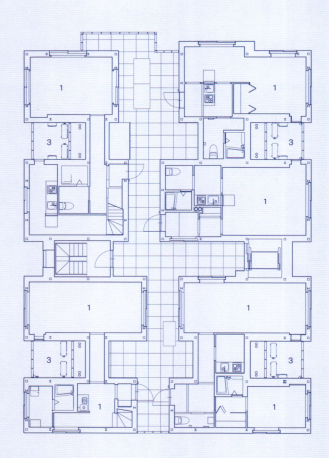

1.2

5F plan | 5F 平面図 | 1:200

088

BUILDING K

1	Shop	1	店舗
2	Room	2	室
3	Equipment space	3	設備スペース
4	Bicycle parking	4	駐輪場

1.2 Section | 断面図 | 1:500

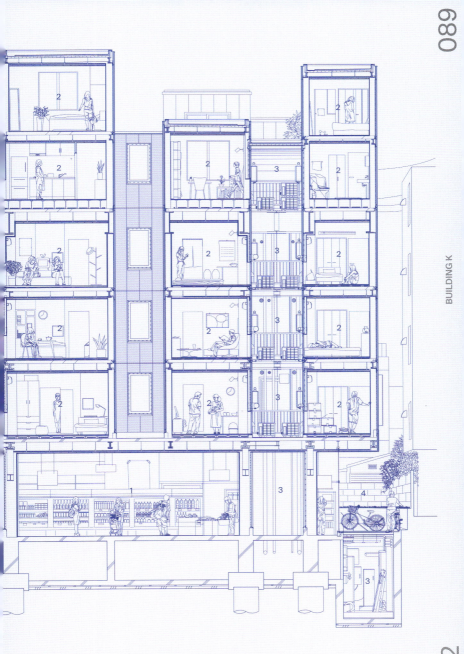

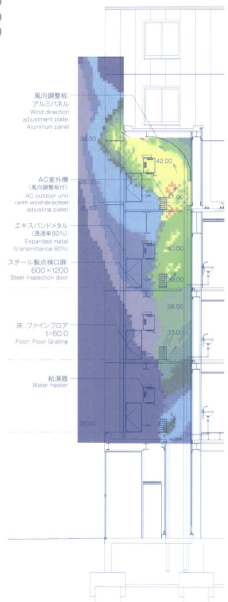

風向調整板:
アルミパネル
Wind direction
adjustment plate:
Aluminum panel

AC室外機
(風向調整板付)
AC outdoor unit
(with wind direction
adjusting plate)

エキスパンドメタル
(透過率80%)
Expanded metal
(transmittance 80%)

スチール製点検口扉:
600×1200
Steel inspection door

床:ファインフロア
t=60.0
Floor: Floor Grating

給湯器
Water heater

● Temperature simulation of the core part (generated in collaboration with the manufacturer).

● コア部分の温度シミュレーション
(メーカーの協力を得て作成)

1.2

BUILDING K

091

● The completed building closely resembles the surrounding townscape but maintains a distinct presence without blending into the background.

● 完成した建築は周囲の風景に限りなく似ているが、
埋没せずに独自性を保つ

1.1

1.2

2.0 | Semiotic Experiments: X HOUSE

2.0　記号をめぐる試行錯誤——○○の家

2.1 Building HOUSE
is a private house like a set of pencil building located in a residential area in the suburb of Tokyo.

After Building K was completed, I spent some time inside the building and found that very pleasant air flows were generated when I opened the small floor-height inspection window for the mechanical duct shaft and the high window at the same time. This finding inspired me to design a house focusing on air flows.

We were commissioned to design a house on a corner site in the suburb of Tokyo, where two roads on the north and east sides intersect at a 120-degree angle. Our design started from placing a large volume deformed to match the site configuration. Then we divided the volume in two and were positioned in parallel with the respective roads. The early model was a combination of a larger volume and a smaller volume, but gradually adjusted it to eliminate the impression of hierarchical relationship between the "main" and "sub" volumes and we ended up with a model comprising a combination of two pencil buildings.

Floor-level windows for natural air supply are concentrated around the V-shaped garden on the north side. Chilled air on the north side enters the building and exits from large-sized high windows on the east and west sides. Air flows that perfectly align with the building orientation are generated by installing ventilation fans concentrated around the exterior void space on the south side. In terms of the window placement, a new order gradually emerged from a disorder through the design process. The garden on the north side was named the "fresh air inlet garden."

It was rather a strange "fiction" to design a house as a set of "pencil buildings." In retrospect, what we presumed at the beginning did not set a direction of design, but what we conceived along the way became a driving force in the latter half of the design process. We started with a model of a

2.1 | ビルの家
は、東京郊外の住宅地に計画された
ビルのような個人住宅である。

―

「BUILDING K」が完成して実際になかで過ごしてみると、設備スペースに面した小さな点検口の地窓(床面に近い窓)を開け、高窓を開けるときに空気が大きく動き、気持ち良く過ごせることに気がついた。そこでもっと空気の動きを手がかりにした住宅を設計してみたいと思った。

―

住宅設計の相談があり、クライアントから示されたのは、東京郊外の住宅地にある、道路が約120度で交わっている交差点に面した角地だった。当初は大きなヴォリュームを敷地のかたちに合わせて変形させていた。やがてヴォリュームをふたつに分け、それぞれの角度を道路の交わる角度に合わせて配置した。当初は片方が大きく、片方が小さかったが、それらがメイン／サブの主従関係に見えたので、それをなくしていくようにしていくと、ふたつのペンシル・ビルが並んだような住宅になった。

―

北側のV字の庭に給気のための地窓を集約した。北側で冷やされた空気はそこから入り、東西に大きく開けられた高窓へ抜けていく。南側の隙間に換気扇を集約させると、空気の流れが建築の配置ときれいに一致する。当初は無秩序だった開口の配列に秩序が生まれていく。北側の庭は「給気口の庭」と名付けた。

―

simple box-shaped volume and then experimentally placed a gable roof on top to make it look like a house, which turned out to be awkward. In the end, we came up with a form that looks as if two "pencil buildings" collided. This form harmonizes with the streetscape of the residential area and also effectively generates air flows coinciding with the building orientation.

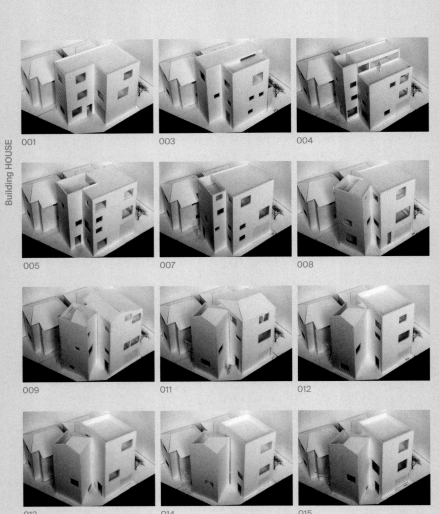

001 003 004
005 007 008
009 011 012
013 014 015

住宅を「ビル」として設計するというフィクションはいささか、奇妙である。振り返ると、設計プロセスの最初に想像されるものが設計をリードすることはないが、途中で想像されるものが設計の後半をリードする。当初はシンプルな箱型のヴォリュームからスタートしたが、途中までは「家」らしく勾配屋根を載せてみたこともあった。でもそれはやはり不自然だと思えて、やがてペンシル・ビルが出合ったかのようなかたちに収束した。そのかたちは住宅地の風景にも、空気の流れと一致させるという機能にも、よりよくなじんでいるように思えた。

016

017

018

019

020

021

022

023

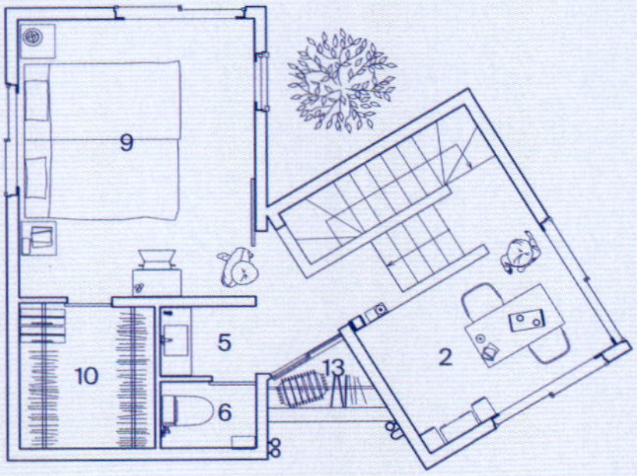

104

Building HOUSE

2.1

1	Entrance
2	Room
3	Bathroom
4	Dressing room
5	Wash room
6	Toilet
7	Living/dining room
8	Kitchen
9	Main bedroom
10	Walk-in closet
11	Air supply garden
12	Equipment space
13	Balcony
14	Parking lot

1	玄関
2	室
3	浴室
4	脱衣所
5	洗面所
6	トイレ
7	リビング・ダイニング
8	キッチン
9	主寝室
10	ウォークインクローゼット
11	給気口の庭
12	設備スペース
13	バルコニー
14	駐車場

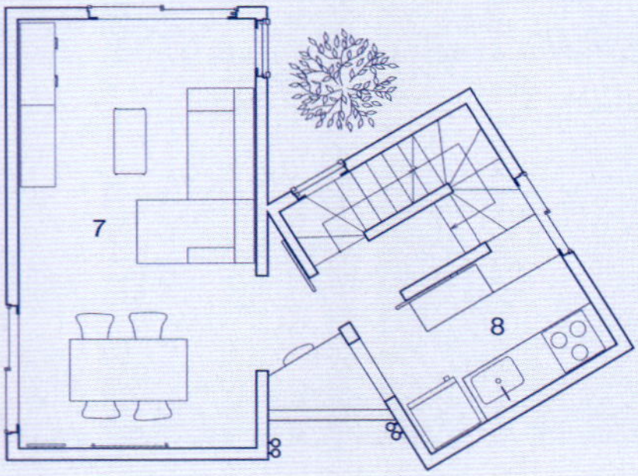

3F plan
3F 平面図
1:150

2F plan
2F 平面図
1:150

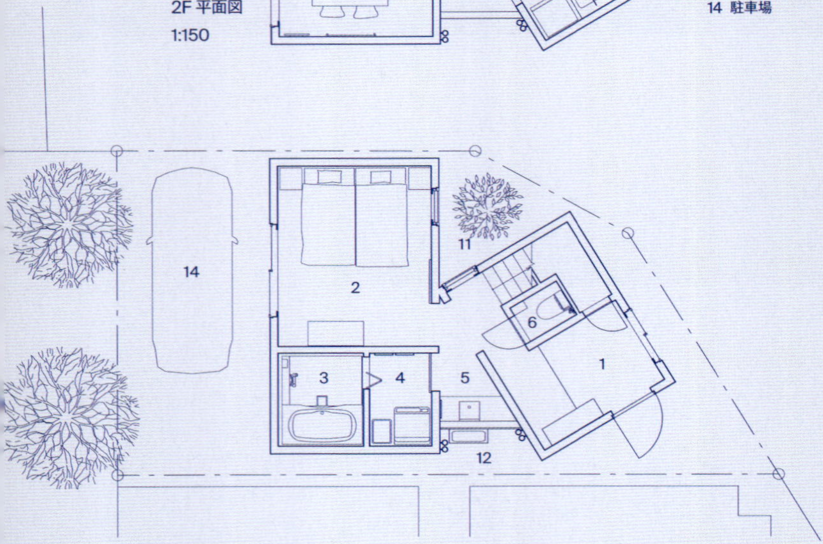

1F plan
1F 平面図
1:150

● Two "buildings" adjoin, rotated at an angle from each other. The gap between the neighboring houses is seen through the gap between the "buildings."

●「ふたつのビル」が角度をもって接するように建つ。隙間から隣と隣の家の隙間が見える

- Windows facing a garden on the north side to let in fresh air.
- 北側の庭に面した窓。空気を取り込む

● Floor-level windows in the bedroom and living room. ● ベッドルームやリビングの足元に開けられた窓

1	Entrance	1	玄関
2	Room	2	室
3	Living/dining room	3	リビング・ダイニング
4	Kitchen	4	キッチン
5	Main bedroom	5	主寝室
6	Air supply garden	6	給気口の庭

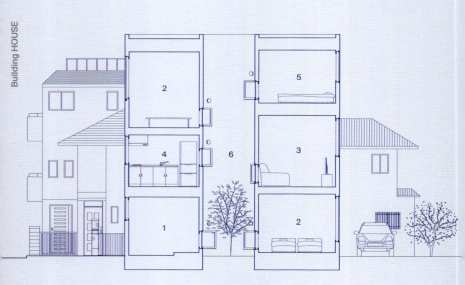

Section｜断面図｜1:150

● The garden on the north side. Air-inlet windows are concentrated around it.

● 給気用の窓が集められた北側の庭

2.1 ヒルの家

2.2 倉庫の家

2.2 | Storage HOUSE
is a private house like a storage located in a residential area in the suburb of Tokyo.

Kanagawa, Japan | 2011
pp.112–131

When a land owner dies, the successor has to pay a large amount of inheritance tax in Japan. In many cases, he/she is forced to sell the land when the tax burden becomes unbearable. For this reason, a land large enough to build a standard-sized house is divided in two or three housing lots to be put up on sale, or similarly designed prefab houses are built on these lots to be put up on sale.

The client's property was one of such small housing lots typical of Tokyo, where the original land was divided in two (in front and back portions). The site is almost fully occupied when a car is parked. A typical layout for this kind of house would be to place a garage, entrance and bathroom on the first floor, a living room on the second floor and a bedroom on the third floor. However, we did not want to impose such a prescribed life style.

The geographical condition presented a breakthrough opportunity. The substrate layer was located at a perfect depth. If we would build a lightweight steel structure above-ground with a concrete basement floor, it would be deep enough to support the structure without pile foundations. Although it would cost more to build a basement floor, the construction cost of two above-ground floors with a basement without pile foundations would be the same as the construction cost of three above-ground floors with pile foundations. In addition, if we build two above-ground floors to reach the maximum allowable height that is high enough for three above-ground floors, we can make the floor height of the first and second floors 1.5 times more than the typical floor height.

Contrary to a typical garage with a minimum ceiling height just enough for a car, we provided a garage with sufficient height and ample natural light like an entrance hall. Place-

2.2 | 倉庫の家
は、東京郊外の住宅地に計画された
倉庫のような個人住宅である。

—

日本では土地の所有者が死亡すると、遺族らが相続する際に多額の税金を支払わなければならない。そのために土地を手放さなければならなくなることが多い。したがって東京の住宅地ではしばしば、住宅1軒が建つ土地がふたつ、3つに分割されて売りに出され、同じような住宅が2、3軒建てられ、販売される。

—

クライアントから示されたのは、そんな東京の住宅地で典型的な、手前と奥に2分割された小さな土地だった。自動車を置くとほとんど空間が残っていない。1階はガレージで奥に玄関と水回り、2階にリビング、3階にベッドルームというのがこの類の住宅の定番である。が、定番どおりに住み方が決められてしまうのは避けたい。

—

突破口になったのは地盤の条件だった。支持層が絶妙な深さにあった。もし地上部を鉄骨で軽くし、地下に部屋を設けると杭を用いずに辛うじて届きそう

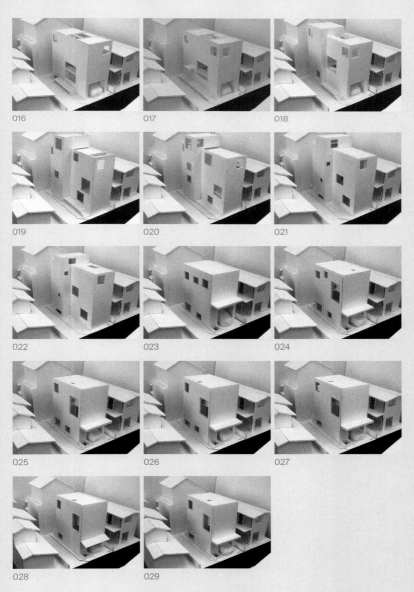

ment of windows had to be determined very carefully to protect the family's privacy in the dense urban environment and the front facade became windowless in the end. A large chimney-like space, connecting the light court in the basement and the void space penetrating through the first and second floors to the roof skylight, distributes sufficient air flows through the entire space.

At the end of the design process, we conceived a house like a storage with a garage, deep eaves and large wall surfaces with few windows, and I named it, "Storage House". The client told us that he likes the name — because he works for a publishing company and feels an affinity with storage.

な深さ。地下に部屋を設けるのはコストがかかるが、地上3階建てを地下1階地上2階建てにして杭を省略できるならばバランスがとれる。地上部は3階分の高さ制限のもとで地上2階にできれば、高さ方向に1.5倍の余裕が生まれることになる。

―

通常は車の高さギリギリに設けるガレージの高さを大きく取った。ガレージはエントランスホールのような、大きく明るい空間になった。周囲は建て込んでいるから窓は慎重に開けなければならない。慎重に、慎重にと窓を減らしているうちに窓はどんどん少なくなり、正面に窓のない家になった。地下室の光庭から吹き抜けを介して屋根のトップライトまで、室内に大きな煙突のような空間をとったところ、室内を大きく空気が流れることとなった。

―

設計を終えて眺めてみると、壁面が大きく、窓が少なく、ガレージとともに大きな庇のある、倉庫のような家だった。そこで私は「倉庫の家」と名付けた。クライアントは出版関係の仕事をしている方だったので、「倉庫は私にとってなじみがあります」と言って気に入ってくれた。

● A garage and dining room, both with the ceiling height 1.5 times more than the average.

● 通常の1.5倍の高さのガレージとダイニング

1	Parking lot	1	駐車場
2	Living/dining room	2	リビング・ダイニング
3	Main bedroom	3	主寝室
4	Room	4	室
5	Storeroom	5	納戸
6	Dressing room	6	脱衣所
7	Corridor	7	廊下
8	Loft	8	ロフト
9	Light court	9	ドライエリア

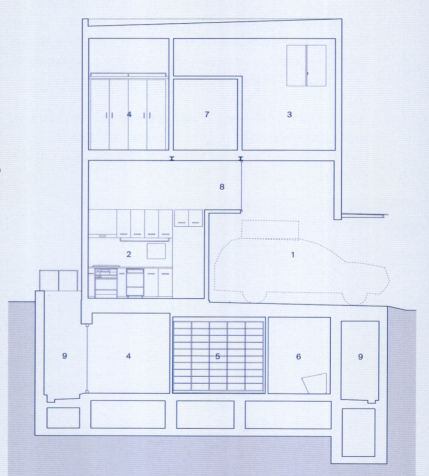

A-A' section | A-A' 断面図 | 1:100

- The garage and balcony are connected through the void that let in light and wind.
- ガレージとバルコニーがつながって光と風を通す

倉庫の家

2.2

1	Living/dining room	1	リビング・ダイニング
2	Storeroom	2	納戸
3	Toilet	3	トイレ
4	Loft	4	ロフト

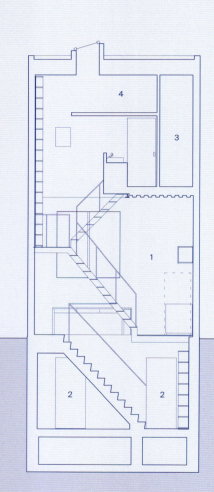

C-C' section | C-C'断面図 | 1:100

● Air entering from the basement ascends. ● 地下階から入った空気が上昇する

1	Garage	1	駐車場
2	Entrance	2	玄関
3	Living/dining room	3	リビング・ダイニング
4	Room	4	室
5	Storeroom	5	納戸
6	Dressing room	6	脱衣所
7	Bathroom	7	浴室
8	Toilet	8	トイレ
9	Storage	9	収納
10	Light court	10	ドライエリア

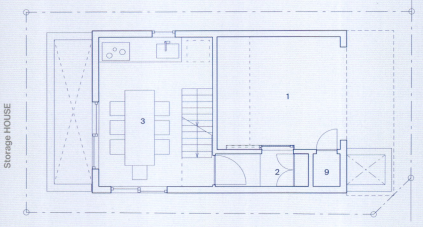

1F plan | 1F 平面図 | 1:100

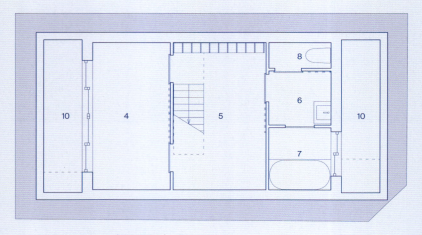

B1F plan | B1F 平面図 | 1:100

● The dining room is located beside a wind passage connecting the basement and the roof.

● ダイニングルームは、
地下から屋上へ
風が抜ける通り道にある

1	Entrance	1	玄関
2	Living/dining room	2	リビング・ダイニング
3	Room	3	室
4	Storeroom	4	納戸
5	Bathroom	5	浴室
6	Balcony	6	バルコニー
7	Storage	7	収納
8	Light court	8	ドライエリア

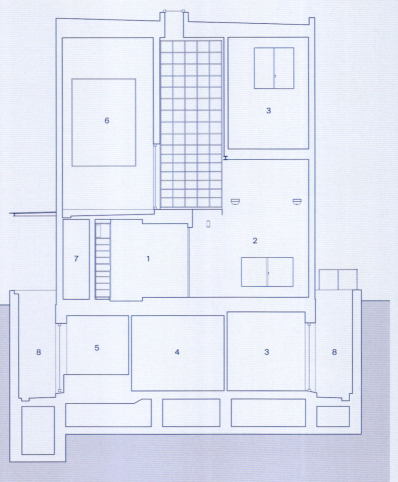

B-B' section ｜ B-B'断面図 ｜ 1:100

● The narrow and tall void simultaneously serves as a book storage and a wind passage.

● 細長い吹き抜けは書庫であり風の通り道でもある

Storage HOUSE

1	Main bedroom
2	Room
3	Toilet
4	Storage
5	Loft
6	Balcony

1	主寝室
2	室
3	トイレ
4	収納
5	ロフト
6	バルコニー

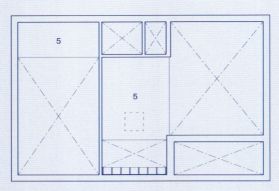

2.5F plan | 2.5F 平面図 | 1:100

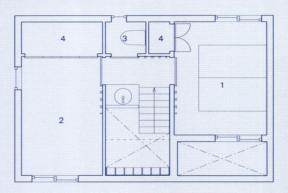

2F plan | 2F 平面図 | 1:100

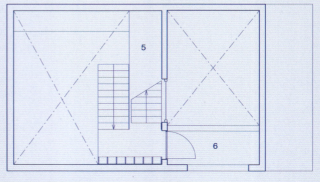

1.5F plan | 1.5F 平面図 | 1:100

● Air ascending from the basement exits through the top light.
● 地下から上昇してきた空気がトップライトから抜ける

倉庫の家

2.3 | Shed HOUSE
is a private house like a shed located in a residential area in the suburb of Tokyo.

I met the client who wanted to build a house on a seaside cliff in the suburb of Tokyo. The site was located on the best spot with an open ocean view towards southwest. I anticipated that finally we would be able to design freely without restrictions, in contrast to the congested inner city area of Tokyo we previously dealt with. After we started designing, however, it turned out that we had various restrictions to consider. It was a steep sloping site with a high water table and the building height had to be lowered as much as possible so as not to obstruct views from the neighbor's house in the back.

If we had designed based on the maximum allowable values imposed by strict restrictions, we would have ended up with a heteronomous house directly shaped by restrictions. On the other hand, autonomous architecture designed without restrictions would have resulted in an articulated form but detached from the context. I was exploring possibilities of realizing architecture that would be shaped autonomously and heteronomously at the same time.

Taking the height limit in to consideration, we built a concrete podium containing a garage and bedroom on the first floor and a wooden hut on the second floor atop the podium. The space is covered with a gently sloped roof supported by a slender column in the center and floor-to-ceiling windows are installed along the southwest side. Partition walls on the second floor are freestanding, and ceiling fans are installed above to circulate air flows from bottom to top.

My idea was to create completely different impressions between the seaside and mountainside — one half of the roof facing the sea is a pitched roof style and the other half facing the mountains is a gabled roof style. Ideally, it would have looked more like a "house" if the gable roof could

2.3 小屋の家
は、東京郊外の住宅地に計画された小屋のような個人住宅である。

東京郊外の海沿いの崖地に住宅を建てたいというクライアントが現れた。西南側に大きく開け、海が見渡せる絶好の土地だった。東京都心部の建て込んだ場所と違って、のびのびと検討ができそうだと感じた。ところがいざ検討を始めてみると、さまざまな制約があった。急な傾斜地、かつ地下水が心配な土地である。また背面の住宅の眺望への配慮から、できるだけ高さを抑えることも求められた。

厳しい制約に対して最大値を取るように設計を行うと、制約のありようを可視化したような、他律的な住宅になる。制約から離れた自律的な建築はかたちが明快だが、コンテクストから離れてしまう。自律的であり他律的でもあるような現れ方を私なりに求めていた。

あまり高さも取れないなら、1階は土留めを兼ねたコンクリートの基壇にガレージとベッドルームを収め、2階部分に木造の小屋を載せることにした。緩い勾配屋根を掛け、鉄骨の細い柱で中心を支え、フルハイトの開口を西南側に設けた。2階の間仕切りは途中までとし、小屋の上部に換気扇を設け、下から上への空気の流れをつくろうとした。

have been raised higher to increase the angle, but unfortunately that wasn't possible. Because the house looked like a small shed built atop a podium, it was named "Shed House." It looks like a mountain shed from the mountain side and a beach shed from the ocean side.

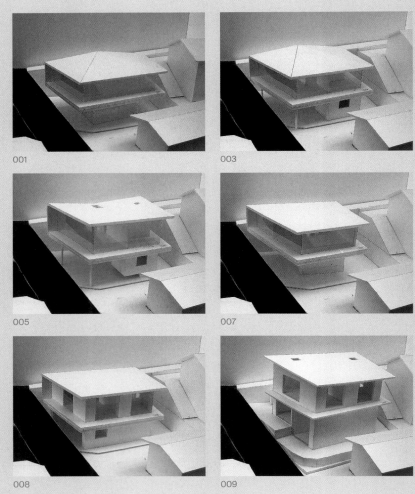

海側は寄棟、山側は切り妻で、両者でまったく異なる表情をもっているのがいいと思った。妻面はもう少し高さが稼げたらより「家」らしいかたちになるのだが、ここでは我慢するしかなかった。基壇の上に建つ小屋のような表情をしていたから「小屋の家」と名付けた。山側から見ると山小屋のようであり、海側から見ると海小屋のようでもある。

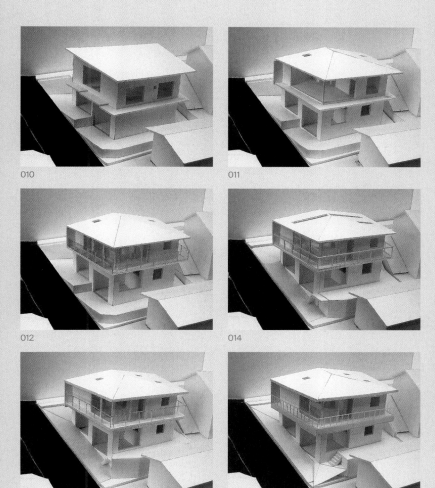

010

011

012

014

015

016

140

Shed HOUSE

2F plan｜2F 平面図
1:150

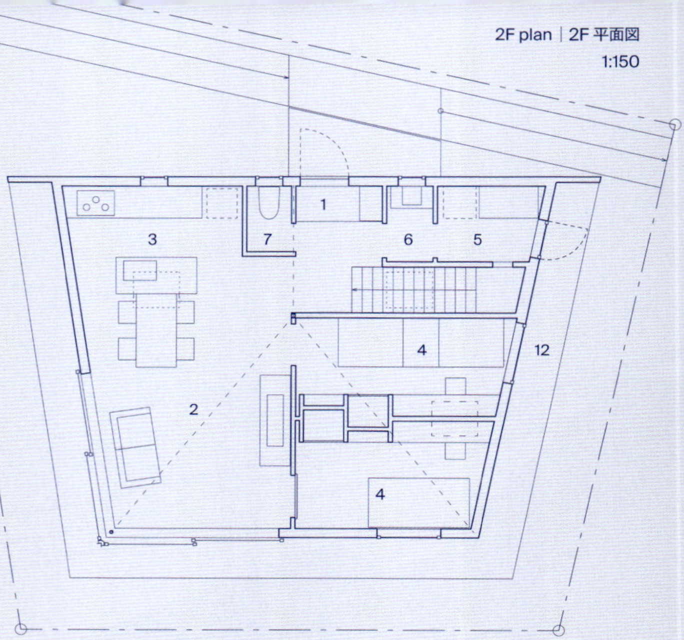

1 Entrance
2 Living/dining room
3 Kitchen
4 Room
5 Utility room
6 Washroom
7 Toilet
8 Main bedroom
9 Walk-in closet
10 Dressing room
11 Bathroom
12 Balcony
13 Garage
14 Equipment space

1F plan｜1F 平面図
1:150

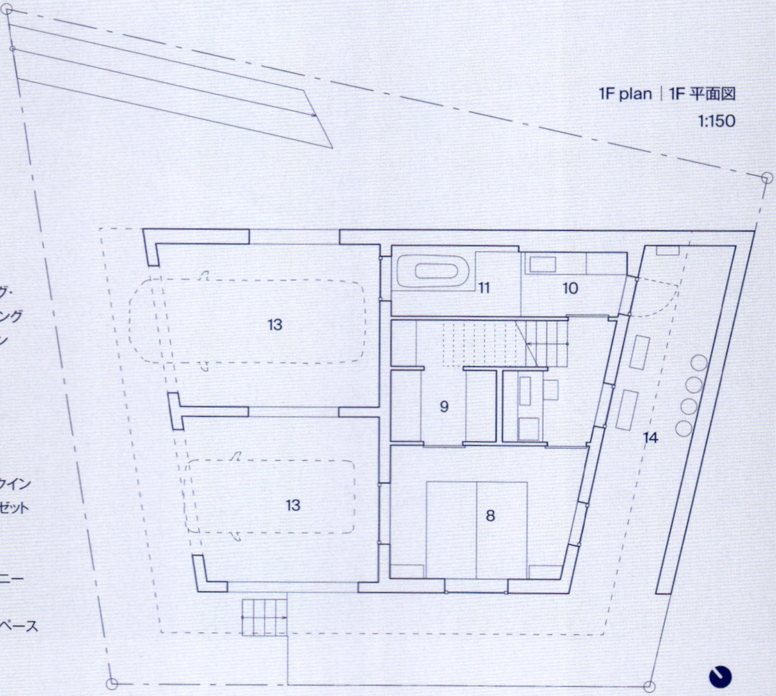

1 玄関
2 リビング・
   ダイニング
3 キッチン
4 室
5 家事室
6 洗面室
7 トイレ
8 主寝室
9 ウォークイン
   クローゼット
10 脱衣所
11 浴室
12 バルコニー
13 車庫
14 設備スペース

2.3

● A living room under the expansive roof accommodates a bedroom enclosed by freestanding walls.

● リビングルームの
おおらかな屋根の下で
壁がベッドルームを区切る

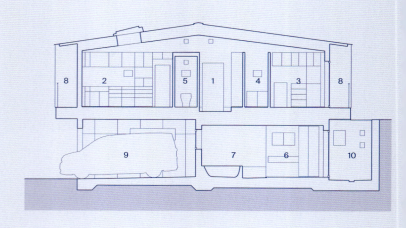

Section | 断面図 | 1:150

1	Entrance	1	玄関
2	Kitchen	2	キッチン
3	Utility room	3	家事室
4	Washroom	4	洗面所
5	Toilet	5	トイレ
6	Dressing room	6	脱衣所
7	Bathroom	7	浴室
8	Balcony	8	バルコニー
9	Garage	9	車庫
10	Equipment room	10	設備スペース

● Relationship between the inclined roof and furniture.

● 勾配屋根と家具の関係

小屋の家

2.3

2.4 | House HOUSE
is a private house like a house located in a residential area in the suburb of Tokyo.

Tokyo, Japan | 2012
pp.146–167

After working on a series of projects under unique conditions, we were commissioned to design a house in a relatively standard condition. The land formerly used for farming was developed into housing lots, and they were starting to construct new houses all at once. This time, the site was a corner lot located in part of a residential area on a level ground, and a house with three or more floors was not considered as a precondition unlike projects in urban sites we have dealt with. I felt that we were finally given a chance to build an "ordinary" two-floor wood house on this site.

We started by placing a box-shaped volume as usual. Then we added a small projecting part to create a garden. After a series of design studies, we opted for an autonomous design approach instead of a heteronomous design approach we usually take. Instead of following our usual method of deciding building dimensions based on the site boundary, we predetermined the main volume as a 6-meter cube and a 6-meter long sub-volume was attached to it. The living room on the first floor turned out to be exactly the same size as the garden. The second floor was divided in four and two 3-meter wide rooms and a bathroom were placed there.

After studying which direction the front facade should face, we decided to orient the gable end towards west. The gable end facade topped with a gently-sloped roof has a floor-height double-sliding window (typically used for a garden/terrace entrance on the ground floor) installed in the center, just below the beam. On the south and north facades, windows are located just below the eaves and directly below the beams.

A two-story wood structure finished with spray wall coating with a gable roof — the house is entirely composed of elements common to the surrounding houses, but arranged

2.4　家の家
は、東京郊外の住宅地に計画された
家のような個人住宅である。

少し特殊な条件での設計が続いていたところへ、比較的オーソドックスな条件で住宅の設計を依頼された。畑として使われていた東京郊外の土地が開発され、新しい住宅群が一斉に建設されようとしていた。今回は都心部のように3階建て以上が前提ではなく、平坦な住宅地の一角、しかも角地だった。ついに木造2階建ての、「普通の」住宅に取り組めそうな敷地に出合うことができた。

いつものように、四角いヴォリュームを置くところから検討を始めた。庭を取りたいと考え、小さな突起を出した。検討を続けた結果、今回はいつものように他律的に解くのではなく、少し自律的に解いてみようと思った。メインヴォリュームの寸法は敷地境界線から追いかけた数値ではなく、6,000mm四方の正方形とした。そこに6,000mmの長さのサブヴォリュームを接続した。1階のリビングと外部の庭が、まったく同じ大きさになった。2階は4分割して3,000mmの部屋をふたつと水回りを置いた。

正面をどちらに取るべきか検討した結果、妻面を西側に向けることにした。緩い勾配屋根を載せた妻面に据えられた窓は、掃き出し窓（1階で出入りにも使われる窓）のプロポーションで2階の中央の、梁がきそうな位置に据えられた。北側と南側の立面の2階には軒にピッタリと付いた、梁を横断しそうな位置に開口がある。

木造2階建て、勾配屋根、吹付け塗装。周りに建っている住宅と構成要素は

House HOUSE

2.4

001

002

003

004

006

007

008

009

010

011

012

013

152

1 Room
2 Toilet
3 Corridor
4 Washroom

1 室
2 トイレ
3 廊下
4 洗面所

House HOUSE

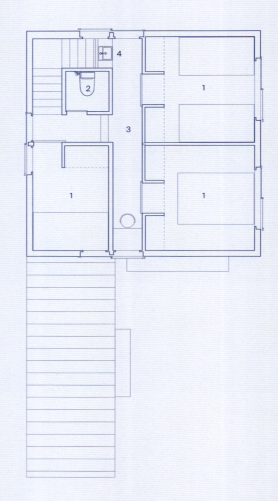

2F plan
2F 平面図
1:100

● 2F plan is composed of a 6,000 x 6,000mm square divided in four sections.

● 6,000mm四方の平面を4分割してできた2階の平面

2.4

154

House HOUSE

2.4

1 Entrance
2 Approach
3 Living/dining room
4 Kitchen
5 Dressing room
6 Bathroom
7 Cloak
8 Toilet
9 Bicycle parking,
  equipment space
10 Garden
11 Parking lot

1 玄関
2 アプローチ
3 リビング・ダイニング
4 キッチン
5 脱衣所
6 浴室
7 クローク
8 トイレ
9 駐輪場, 設備スペース
10 庭
11 駐車場

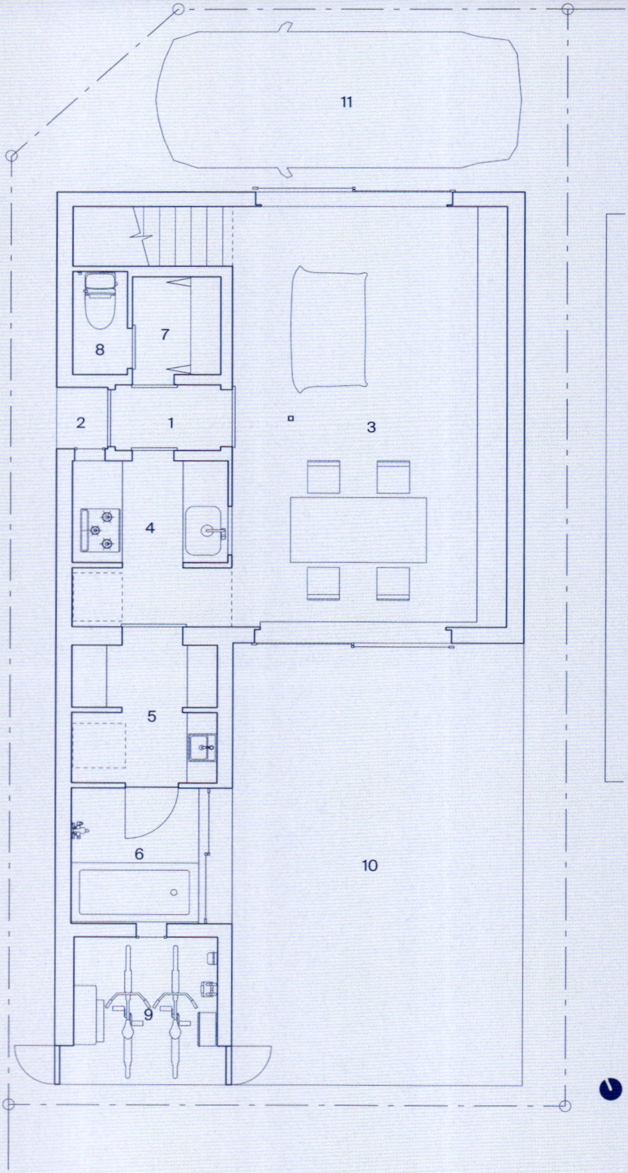

1F plan
1F 平面図
1:100

● 1F plan is composed of a 6,000
x 6,000mm square adjoining a
6,000mm-wide sub-volume.

● 6,000mm四方の平面に
6,000mmのサブヴォリュームを
接続してできた1階の平面

in a slightly different way from the conventional style. Such slight differences seem to evoke a sense of freedom throughout the house. This is a contemporary approach — and a Japanese or a Tokyo suburban approach — to the same theme Robert Venturi addressed in the Vanna Venturi House.

I wondered what kind of theme we should set for this house, after dealing with themes such as "building", "storage", and "shed" in the previous projects. "House House" seemed to be the only and most appropriate name of the house. It is a "critical house" conceived through the process of reanalyzing conventions in a new light and carefully recomposing elements constituting a "house". I was convinced that we successfully designed a new suburban house prototype that can be adopted in the coming future.

まったく同じである。だが、配列が慣習的なものとちょっとだけ違うようにつくられた住宅である。しかしそのささいなズレが生み出す自由さが全体に満ちていると感じた。ロバート・ヴェンチューリが「母の家」で取り組んだテーマの現代版。そして日本版、あるいは東京郊外版である。

「ビル」「倉庫」「小屋」ときて、この家は何だろうと考えた。「家の家」としか呼びようのない住宅に見えた。慣習を読み解き、「家」を構成する要素を丁寧に与え直した、「批判的な家(critical house)」である。今後、日本の郊外住宅地で住宅を設計するための、ひとつのプロトタイプを設計できたような気がした。

161

家の家

2.4

● Bedrooms are enclosed by freestanding walls under the expansive roof, and the accumulated hot air is blown to the lower floor.

● おおらかな屋根の下で壁がベッドルームを区切り、溜まった熱気を下階に吹き下ろす

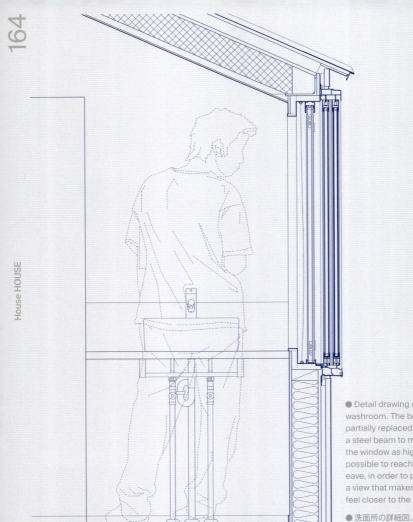

● Detail drawing of the washroom. The beam is partially replaced with a steel beam to make the window as high as possible to reach the eave, in order to provide a view that makes one feel closer to the sky.

● 洗面所の詳細図。
梁の一部を鉄骨に置き換え、窓を軒に近づけることで空が近くなる

Detailed section | 断面詳細図 | 1:15

● The house is built of the same materials as the neighboring houses but designed to give a more compact and abstract impression.

● 周囲の住宅と同じ材料を使いながら、小さく、抽象的に構える

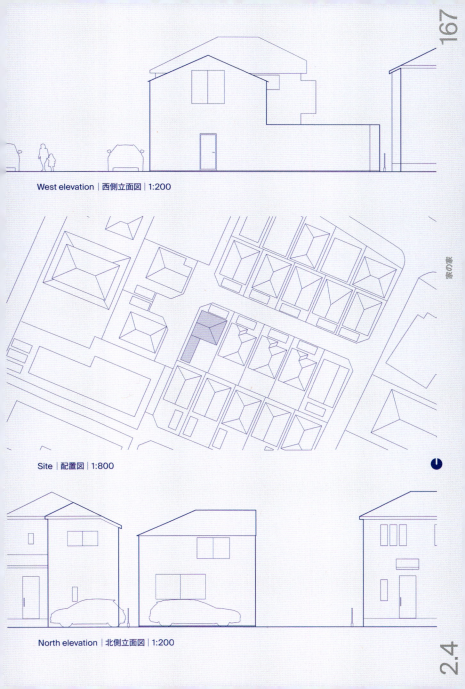

West elevation｜西側立面図｜1:200

Site｜配置図｜1:800

North elevation｜北側立面図｜1:200

168 | 3.0 | Mass Learning, Mass Decision

Evolutional Process of Single Option
単線の進化的プロセス

Evolutional Process of Several Options
複線の進化的プロセス

Evolutional and Integral Process of Several Options
進化的かつ統合的なプロセス

3.0 集団で学ぶこと、集団で決めること

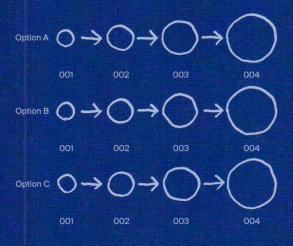

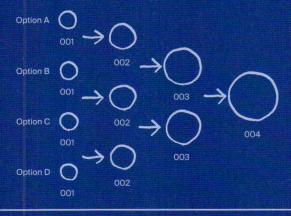

3.1 | Tsurugashima Project
is a new approach to administrative problem-solving by publically presenting university students'design proposals for a public facility.

In autumn of 2008, I started teaching design studio at a university and gave students an assignment for the first time. It was a time when the effect of the financial crisis that had struck in the United States spread to the rest of the world and Barak Obama won the presidential election. The demands of the society started to shift drastically from efficiency to diversity.

I started teaching as a full-time lecturer in spring of 2010. The department of architecture had 140 students and 10 teachers per class, and the students were divided into ten groups to be taught by respective teachers. The teachers were from diverse backgrounds and generations: both emerging and experienced; male and female; and architects and researchers. The design studio displayed considerable diversity due to the fact that each teacher was teaching at his/her discretion, but students seemed somewhat confused by such diversity from an educational point of view. The source of confusion was mainly arbitrary evaluation criteria — it wasn't clear what is good or bad, whether a certain project was highly evaluated for the quality of the model or the proposal itself or whether evaluation was based on the teacher's personal preference or objective criteria.

In order to solve this problem, I started to incorporate a public interest point of view in the design studio and invited the Mayor of Tsurugashima-city to take part in it: he would give students an assignment; students would present their proposals to him; and he would evaluate their proposals. The students present their ideas to an interested party who had issues to deal with, and not to the teachers. I remembered that the Berlage Institute in the Netherlands, where I studied, had implemented similar experimental methods in design studios from the 1990's to 2000's.

| 3.1 | 鶴ヶ島プロジェクト
は、大学生がパブリックミーティングで
公共施設の設計案を提示し、
行政の課題解決を図る試みである。

2008年の秋、私は初めて大学の設計を教えるスタジオで課題を出題した。アメリカを起点に世界中で金融危機が起こり、バラク・オバマが大統領に選ばれようとしていた頃だ。効率性から多様性へ、社会の求めるものが変わろうとしていた。

2010年春から、私はある大学で専任の教員として教え始めていた。その大学では140名の学生を10名の教員で、10のグループに分けて教育していた。10名の教員にはベテランもいれば若手も、男性もいれば女性も、建築家もいれば研究者もいる。それぞれの教員がそれぞれの裁量で指導をし、多様性があった。ただ、教育としては少々学生を混乱させているようにも思えた。何が良くて何が良くないのか、優れているのは模型の出来栄えなのか案そのものなのか、教員の好みなのか客観的な指標に基づいての評価なのか、専門家としての判断なのか利用者の判断なのかなど、原因は主に評価の問題であった。

ならばと始めたのは、市長に課題を出題してもらい、市長にプレゼンして評価を

In spring of 2012, I had an opportunity to discuss public architecture with architects in Switzerland. At the discussion, I learned that the city of Basel in Switzerland mandated a regulation regarding the selection process of an architect for a public facility project, which require participating architects to submit a 1/500 model along with drawings and the decision is made according to the result of direct voting by local residents. In addition, competition organizers should prepare site models by themselves in order to eliminate unnecessary differences and each participant is requested to buy one, as he/she is required to place a model of his/her proposed building on the site model for submission. I learned that it is important to prepare a proper format in order to fairly evaluate diverse proposals. This new knowledge inspired me to introduce this Swiss method to our design studio in Japan.

We incorporated public meetings in our design studio and students' proposals were evaluated based on the results of public voting. Only higher-rank winners can proceed to a public presentation and discussion where another public voting is held to determine the final winner of the day. The meeting was held once every two weeks and was repeated five times. The students' works were evaluated not by teachers but by visitors. Before voting, visitors hear comments from relevant professionals before and after the vote. The vote takes place not just once but multiple times.

When applying this method, we often see similar proposals but they are often evaluated differently depending on vote results. Rivals influence each other by observing how a particular proposal is highly or lowly evaluated. Both parties — those who make proposals and those who evaluate them — learn together through these procedures. This is not a typical design competition or voting. Architecture is a place to practice democracy.

してもらうという当事者感覚の導入であった。学生は教員に向けてプレゼンを行うのではなく、課題を抱えている当事者に向けてプレゼンを行う。私が留学していたオランダのベルラーヘ・インスティテュートでは1990年代から2000年代にかけてそのような試みが行われていたことを思い出した。

—

2012年の春、スイスで建築家と公共建築について議論する機会があった。スイスのバーゼルでは公共施設の設計者を選ぶ際に図面とともに1/500の模型を提出し、住民が直接投票するようになったという話を聞いた。敷地の模型も余計な差がつかないよう主催者が用意するものを応募者が購入し、提案部分を当てはめて提出するそうだ。多様性を評価するために、フォーマットをしっかりと整える。私はこのスイスの方法を日本に導入したいと思うようになった。

—

演習にパブリックミーティングを組み込み、学生の提案に来場者が投票を行う。投票で上位に残ったものがプレゼンと意見交換に進むことができる。そして再度投票を行い、その日の順位を確定する。これを2週間に1回、5回繰り返す。評価を行うのは教員ではなく一般来場者。ただし投票の前後に専門家がコメントを入れる。投票を一度ではなく複数回行う。

—

複数の案が並行する。投票によって評価が分かれる。ある案に対する評価が高まったり、低かったりすることでライバルが影響を受け、そして与えていく。提案者も、評価者も、ともに学んでいく。これは単なるコンペでも、単なる投票でもない。建築とは、新しい民主主義の練習の場である。

● A public meeting at the project site, where we addressed issues to the public.

● 現場で、当事者に向かって課題を訴えるパブリックミーティング

● The fifth project meeting (18 July 2012)　　● 第5回目のパブリックミーティング（2012年7月18日）

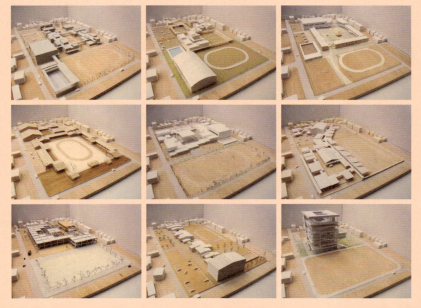

● A symposium held at the city hall. An exhibition at Shibuya Hikarie. Newspaper articles featuring our project. Actions to stir up public opinions.

● 市役所でのシンポジウム、渋谷ヒカリエでの展覧会、新聞への掲載。世論をつくる

bottom left: The Nihon Keizai Shinbun, 18 February 2014, p.9, Tokyo, Japan: Nikkei, Inc.
左下:『日本経済新聞』2014年2月18日 夕刊 9面

- A construction schedule proposing when and how reduction of all public facilities owned by the city should be implemented.
- 市が保有する公共施設全体をいつ、どのように縮小していくかの工程表

中学校は規模適正化・

New Unifie
Optimization of junior high school capacity. Aggressive reduction of el

番号(No)	地区(Area)	施設(Facility)	名称(Name)	1960 1970 1980 1990 2000 2010
①	A地区 A Area	小学校 Elementary School	a小学校 a Elementary School	竣工|Completion (1969)　　1994■　2001☐　469人|
			b小学校 b Elementary School	竣工|Completion (1980)　　　　2008☐　407人|
		中学校 Junior High School	a中学校 a Junior High School	竣工|Completion (1977)　　　2006☐　447人|
		市民センター Civic Center	a市民センター a Civic Center	竣工|Completion (1985)
②	B地区 B Area	小学校 Elementary School	c小学校 c Elementary School	竣工|Completion (1969)　　1994■　2002☐　287人|
			bセンター b Civic Center	竣工|Completion (1984)
③	C地区 C Area	小学校 Elementary School	d小学校 d Elementary School	竣工|Completion (1978)　　　　749人|
		中学校 Junior High School	b中学校 b Junior High School	竣工|Completion (1985)　　　　408人|
		市民センター Civic Center	c市民センター c Civic Center	竣工|Completion (2002)
④	D地区 D Area	小学校 Elementary School	e小学校 e Elementary School	竣工|Completion (1979)　　　　482人|
			f小学校 f Elementary School	竣工|Completion (1980)　2006☐　403人|
		中学校 Junior High School	c中学校 c Junior High School	竣工|Completion (1980)　2009☐　263人|
		市民センター Civic Center	d市民センター d Civic Center	竣工|Completion (1981)
			e市民センター e Civic Center	竣工|Completion (1987)
⑤	E地区 E Area	小学校 Elementary School	g小学校 g Elementary School	竣工|Completion (1983)　　　　512人|
		中学校 Junior High School	d中学校 d Junior High School	竣工|Completion (1979)　2009☐　533人|
⑥	F地区 F Area	小学校 Elementary School	h小学校 h Elementary School	竣工|Completion (1985)　　　　426人|
		中学校 Junior High School	e中学校 e Junior High School	竣工|Completion (1985)　　　　280人|
		市民センター Civic Center	f市民センター f Civic Center	竣工|Completion (1991)

- 小学校 | Elementary School
- 中学校 | Junior High School
- 市民センター | Civic Center
- ■ 大規模改修 | Large-Scale Repair

➡ 利活用(築75年までを想定)
Utilization (subject to buildings up to 75 years old)

1981.6
確認申請
新耐震基準
Application for building confirmation
new earthquake resistance standards

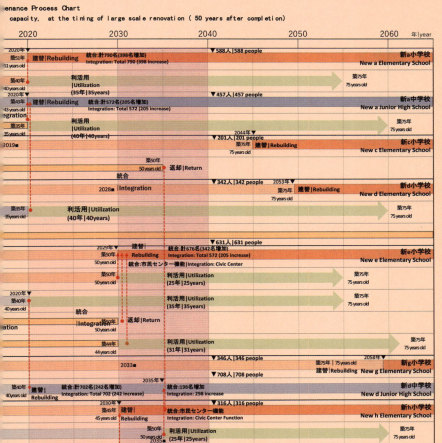

● Elementary School District (8 Schools)

● 小学校区（8区）

● Insured Long-Term Care Service Plans, Daily Life Area

● 介護保険事業計画日常生活圏域

● Supporting Council Area

● 支え合い協議会区分

● Re-planning of the placement of all public facilities owned by the city. This proposal pointed out the existing disorganized state of boundaries between elementary schools, communities, and welfare and proposed reorganization of the boundaries. It is necessary to redraw maps so that architecture functions most effectively. This is a map for reduction.

● 市が保有する公共施設全体の配置をやり直す。小学校、コミュニティ、福祉の境界線がバラバラであったのを再統一する提案。建築を本当に機能させるためには、地図を描き直す必要がある。縮小のための地図

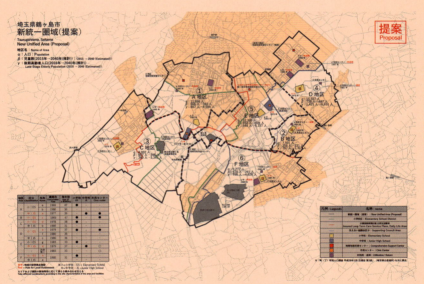

● New Unified Area (Proposal)
● 新統一圏域(提案)

3.2 Facility for Ecology Education
is an experimental design project in which design proposals by ten graduate school students are shared publicly throughout the design process.

While the Tsurugashima Project was in full swing, another project was progressing on the adjacent site. They were planning a solar power plant comprising solar panels laid out on a brownfield land of a former factory site. After the Great East Japan Earthquake in March 2011, Japan's energy policy, which had largely relied on nuclear power generation, was revised and solar power plants were increasingly considered as a potential replacement. The former factory site in the suburb was a perfect location for a solar power plant due to low housing demand in the area. Some people, however, questioned the feasibility of building such a large-scale solar power plant in the residential area.

Our experimental approach in the Tsurugashima Project caught much attention as an effective way of communicating with and engaging local residents. Incidentally, ten of my former undergraduate students who had participated in the project had just entered graduate school then. I came up with an idea of assigning them as leaders of the design process in which a series of public meetings and votes woud be conducted.

Even though the building we were planning was named "Facility for Ecology Education", its contents had not been specified. While one can clearly picture what people would do in a facility like an elementary school or hospital, it is difficult to imagine what people would do in a new type of facility like this. Only the total floor area and the budget had been decided for the time being. I was concerned that residents wouldn't be able to voice their opinions in such uncertain situations. We therefore devised a design method where students would serve in a role of an architect and present proposals to residents several times. This way, we would be able to incorporate the residents' opinions at each step and

3.2 鶴ヶ島太陽光発電所環境教育施設
は、大学院生10名の案を公開しながら、
環境教育施設の設計を行う試みである。

「鶴ヶ島プロジェクト」が盛り上がっていた頃、ちょうど隣の敷地で別のプロジェクトが進んでいた。工場跡地のブラウンフィールドに太陽光パネルを並べ、発電所にする計画である。2011年3月の東日本大震災のあとで原子力発電に依存したこれまでの日本のエネルギー政策が見直され、太陽光発電所が注目されていた。郊外の工場跡地には住宅需要も少ないため、太陽光発電所の設置にはぴったりであった。ただし、住宅地にそんな大きな太陽光発電所をつくってもいいのか、疑問視する声もあった。

周辺住民と対話し、巻き込む手段として、私たちの試みが着目された。ちょうど「鶴ヶ島プロジェクト」に取り組んだ大学生たちが10名、大学院に進学していた。彼らが主役となってパブリックミーティングで投票を行いながら設計するプロセスはどうだろうかと思いついた。

計画中の施設には「環境教育施設」という名称がつけられていたが、内容はあまり具体化されていなかった。小学校や病院であれば何をする場所なのか想

184

Facility for Ecology Education

3.2

Design Participants 設計参加者	The initial plans 初期案（001案）	The 1st public meeting 第1回パブリックミーティング 2013.5.11	The 2nd public meeting 第2回パブリックミーティング 2013.5.25
A 赤岩駿也 Shunya Akaiwa	001-A	002-A / 3 votes/票	003-A / 3 votes/票
B 梓澤亜美 Tsugumi Azusawa	001-B	002-B / 4 votes/票	003-B / 1 votes/票
C 熊井康博 Yasuhiro Kumai	001-C	002-C / 6 votes/票	003-C / 11 votes/票
D 倉上将徳 Yukinori Kurakami	001-D	002-D / 0 votes/票	003-D / 0 votes/票
E 坂本庄平 Kyohei Sakamoto	001-E	002-E / 8 votes/票	003-E / 13 votes/票
F 塩澤大 Hiroshi Shiosawa	001-F	002-F / 5 votes/票	003-F / 4 votes/票
G 嶋田裕紀 Hironori Shimada	001-G	002-G / 0 votes/票	003-G / 4 votes/票
H 高橋杏介 Kyosuke Takahashi	001-H	002-H / 10 votes/票	003-H / 3 votes/票
I 友國樹伸 Tatsunobu Tomokuni	001-I	002-I / 8 votes/票	003-I / 6 votes/票
J 西村岐 Shun Nishimura	001-J	002-J / 3 votes/票	003-J / 4 votes/票

像がつくが、新しい施設なので、何をするところかよくわからない。とりあえず全体の面積と予算だけが決まっていた。その状態で住民に意見を求めても、何を意見すればよいかわからないだろうと思われた。そこで学生が建築家の役を務め、複数の案を複数回提示する。その過程で住民の意見を反映すると同時に、どうしたら彼らを巻き込めるか、議論をすることができると考えた。

—

ここでもまた、彼らのつくる模型が役に立った。ここで見せる模型は、建設予定のものを細密に再現するジオラマとは違い、「その時点で確かだと思えること」をとりあえずかたちにしたプロトタイプである。全体の予算は決まっているが、必要な部屋のリストも、面積表もない。自治体と民間企業が資金を出し合う複合施設なので、誰がメインの発注者なのかもよくわからない。そんなときに、例えば敷地のかたち、面積、配置、屋根のかたちなど、とりあえず確かだと思えることをかたちにしてみる。それをパブリックミーティングで提示して投票してもらいながら、何が課題なのかを探っていくのである。

—

10案の模型を提示する。するとどういうわけかゼロ票の提案がある。よく見ると、共通して2階建ての提案である。投票のあとでヒアリングすると、近所の自治会館が2階建てで階段の昇り降りにお年寄りが困っているのだという。そこで次回から「2階建てはNG」というルールが設計者にフィードバックされる。このように初めから「平屋限定」とわかっていなくても、かたちにしてみたら「それはダメ」という項目が見つかることがある。このようなやりとりを何度か繰り返すことで、設計の前提条件が明らかになることがある。

—

デザインという作業は、与件をすべて明らかにしてスタートするものとは限らない。むしろ新しい課題は、かたちにしてみないと見えてこないことがある。住民意見を聴く期間がしっかり設けられていたのにもかかわらず、建築工事が始まってから反対の声が上がることもあるのは、かたちになって初めて住民は事の重大さを知るからである。市民に意見をヒアリングして「コンセプト」をまとめ、「かたち」はデザイナーに任せましょう、というプロセスがときに不自然に映るのも、デザイナーがかたちにしたものを見ないと、事の本質がわからないからである。

● Ten proposals presented by graduate school students. The community's needs were gradually identified by repeating voting. Assistant: Kazuki Shiohara

● 大学院生たちが提示した10個の設計案。投票を繰り返しながらニーズを理解する
アシスタント：塩原和記

discuss how to get them involved in the design process.

Models made by students served as an effective communication tool once again. These models were ad hoc prototypes based on what we know for sure at that point, and not detailed dioramas of buildings to be constructed. While the overall budget already had been decided, the client didn't have a list of room requirements or floor area table. Because the local authority and the private company would split the construction cost of this educational complex, we were not sure who the main client was. Under such circumstances, we made models based on what we knew for sure — namely the site configuration, floor areas, placement, roof shape and so on. Students presented these models at each public meeting and discussed what issues we needed to deal with based on the result of the voting.

When we presented models of ten design proposals, some of the proposals got zero vote for some reason. We took a second look and realized that they were all two-story buildings. We had a public hearing after the voting and learned that the residents' association hall in the neighborhood is a two-story building and that the elderly residents were having difficulties going up and down the stairs. Based on the feedback, we started to apply a new design rule that "two-story buildings are not acceptable" at the next meeting. Even though we were not aware that only a one-story building would be acceptable in the beginning, some unacceptable conditions became clear through communication using physical models. Preconditions for design are often clarified by repeating this communication method.

All necessary conditions are not always clear when we start designing. On the contrary, we often find new issues after we transform our ideas into physical forms. Residents often express disapproval of a public building after construction has started, even when they had opportunities to express opinions at public hearings before construction. This is because they can recognize serious consequences of the construction only after they see the design in a physical form. The design process carried out by firstly setting "design concepts" based on public hearings and then having a

鶴ヶ島太陽光発電所環境教育施設

designer decide its "form" often seems awkward, because most people don't understand the essence of design until they see it in a physical form.

Reduction and Form

We learned another important lesson through this construction project. It was regarding the question of how to achieve common understanding of the gap between ideal and reality, namely the difference between the total required volume and the maximum buildable volume within the budget, between all parties in the collective design process. Generally, the client reviews all requests in advance and adjusts the overall volume to fit within the budget limit before placing order for design work. However, high level of communication is inevitable in the case of group order and collective design.

In the Facility for Ecology Education project, the required volume greatly exceeded the maximum buildable volume within the budget in the beginning. Each department of the local authority and the private company made specific requests separately — including a power plant janitor's room, ecological education classroom for school children, exhibition room for a railroad diorama made by a local company and so on. Moreover, each department wanted a dedicated toilet and kitchen so that they can maintain them individually.

It would be easy to start a discussion as soon as problems like these are found when working on a one-on-one basis between the client and the architect. On the contrary, it is difficult to find the right person to negotiate with when designing a multifunctional facility in collaboration with multiple parties. It seems that a similar problem happened in Japan's New National Stadium design competition in which Zaha Hadid had been initially involved. In general, people tend to blame architects for going way over budget presumably due to his/her "egoistic design."

● A cost reduction workshop. People did not only give requests but also discussed which requests to eliminate.

● 減額ワークショップ。要望を出すだけでなく、減らすところを議論する

縮小とかたち

実施プロジェクトならではの学びはもうひとつあった。集団で設計する時に、要求のヴォリュームと、予算の範囲内で実現できるヴォリュームのギャップをどのように共有するかという問題である。本来ならば発注者が事前に要求を整理しておいて、予算におおまかに収まるように全体の面積を調整をした上で設計の発注がなされるべきであるが、集団で発注し、集団で設計する場合だと、そのコミュニケーションに工夫が要求される。

「鶴ヶ島太陽光発電所環境教育施設」のプロジェクトでも、当初は関係者から要求されている面積の合計が予算内で実現できる面積をはるかに上回っていた。発電所の管理人が常駐する部屋と、市内の児童が訪れ環境について学ぶための部屋、鶴ヶ島市内にある企業が製造している鉄道模型を展示する部屋、というように、自治体と企業、それぞれの部署がばらばらに要求していたからである。しかもそれぞれ別々に管理できるように、トイレもキッチンも別々にほしいという。

発注者と設計者が1対1であればそのような問題が見つかればすぐに交渉することができる。ところが、いくつかの機能を複合化した施設の設計プロセスでは、誰が発注の責任者なのか曖昧になり交渉の相手が誰だかわからない。ザハ・ハディドが関わった新国立競技場でも同じ問題が起こっていたようだ。予

Considering such situations, we took a rather tricky procedure of studying ten options and narrowed them down to three options by grouping together options by common characteristics, and then strategically presented to the audience estimates of construction costs of respective options. After taking a vote and carrying out discussion regarding the three options, we showed them the cost estimates and said, "These are the cost estimates incorporating all your requests." In fact, all of the cost estimates turned out to be more than double the budget and as a result, we were able to verify that they were making too many requests that were way over budget.

In the public meeting, I asked them, "Which request do you think should be omitted, then?" I called this experimental approach the "cost reduction workshop." People are accustomed to giving requests, but not reducing them. Public workshops generally present opportunities for citizens to freely express themselves, but sometimes make them lose a sense of humbleness. We wanted to show that "limits" of a project could be visualized in physical forms by expressing our ideas in models.

Takashi Asada at Kenzo Tange Laboratory wisely stated that "the essence of design emerges in the cost estimate adjustment process." We can start the cost reduction process to discuss which request to eliminate only when the estimated amount greatly exceeds the budget. It would be better to have several options to compare when deciding which element is important or unnecessary in design proposals. I learned that this kind of methodology is called an "option approach" in policy studies.

算をオーバーしたのは勝手なデザインをした建築家が悪いのだ、と建築家のせいにされかねない。
―

そこで私たちは、少々アクロバティックであるが、10個のオプションを共通の特徴をもつ3つのオプションに絞った段階で、それぞれに対する見積り額を公開する作戦を採った。3つのオプションに投票と意見交換を行ったあとで「皆さんのご希望を叶えるようにするとこれだけの金額になります」と金額を示したのである。どの案も予定の2倍以上だった。すべてのオプションの見積り額がオーバーしていたことで、原因はデザインによって生まれたものではなく、要求が多すぎることだったことがわかる。
―

パブリックミーティングで「さてどこを削りましょう」と問いかけた。私はこの試みを「減額ワークショップ」と名付けた。私たちは要求を出すことには慣れていても、要求を減らすことには慣れていない。ワークショップは市民を自由にするが、ときとして謙虚さを失わせる。アイデアを模型にすることで、プロジェクトが担うべきリミットを「かたち」にすることもできることを示したかった。
―

「設計の本質は見積り調整にあり」とは丹下研究室の浅田孝の至言である。見積額が予算を大幅に上回ったときに初めて、ようやくどの要望を削るかを議論できる。そのプロセスで案のなかのどの要素が大事でどの要素が大事でないかを区別することができる。そのとき、いくつかのオプションがあると良い。そのような方法論を政策論では「オプション・アプローチ」というらしい。

192

3.2 Facility for Ecology Education

3.2 鶴ヶ島太陽光発電所環境教育施設

Symbol and Form

Would it be possible to reduce the size of a building but still keep the design idea, instead of reducing the design idea altogether? In the process of narrowing down the options to three, we took a purely constructive approach of grouping options by common characteristics, articulating elements comprising each characteristic and classified them into different types. Hence, the three options inherit formal characteristics of the ten options. I gave names to the three options: the first one is the "church type" comprising a symbolic roof and a symmetric plan, the second one is the "station type" comprising a gently-inclined roof and a gate-shaped site plan, and the third one is the "alley type" comprising a space on an intimate scale and equipped with benches. The "station type" won the most popular vote.

If we were to select the most popular proposal, the opinions of people supporting other proposals would be ignored. In my view, voting should be considered as an effective means to bring out one's sense of agency and the "majority rule" in decision making should not apply. After the vote, we held a public hearing and asked each participant the reasons for selecting a particular proposal and gained a better understanding of their needs.

After the "cost reduction workshop", we eliminated excessive elements and provided shared toilets and rooms where possible, while keeping key components which people

記号とかたち

ヴォリュームを小さくしていくときに、アイデアを削るのではなく、アイデアは保存したままサイズだけを小さくすることはできないか。オプションを3つに絞る際に、得られた3つのオプションは、特徴を整理し、それぞれの特徴を構成する要素を明らかにした上で類型化するという、極めて構成論的なアプローチを採った。従って3つのオプションはかたちのレベルで10案の特徴を構成する要素をそれぞれ引き継いでいる。私は3つの案にそれぞれ名前をつけた。ひとつは象徴的な屋根とシンメトリーの平面形をもつ「教会型」。もうひとつはやさしい勾配屋根でゲート型の配置を採った「駅舎型」。もうひとつは親しみのあるスケールで街路を引き込みベンチを備えた「路地型」である。投票では「駅舎型」の人気が高かった。

The 3rd public meeting
第3回パブリックミーティング
2013.6.22

The 4th public meeting
第4回パブリックミーティング
2013.7.13

004-Station type | A+C+H | 43 votes
Elements
1. The angle of solar panels
2. Sense of a gate
3. Semi-external space

004-駅舎型 | A+C+H | 43票
構成要素
1. 太陽光パネルの角度
2. ゲート性
3. 半外部空間

004-Church type | E+G+I | 19 votes
Elements
1. Symbolic
2. Plaza
3. A line of visual access penetrating through it

004-教会型 | E+G+I | 19票
構成要素
1. 象徴性
2. 広場
3. 視線の貫通

005-Integrated-type | 005-統合型

004-Alley type | B+D+F+J | 17 votes
Elements
1. Separated structures
2. Benches
3. Draws a passageway into it

004-路地型 | B+D+F+J | 17票
構成要素
1. 分棟
2. ベンチ
3. 通路の引き込み

● The final proposal was created based on three selected design proposals. We made sure that their characteristics were somehow incorporated.

● 大きく3つに絞り込まれた設計案の特徴を殺さずに最終案をつくる

mentioned as part of their reasons for selecting a particular proposal and incorporating them in the facility. The final proposal was carefully designed so that all of the key components that were highly evaluated in the three proposals would remain. The three proposals had been determined in such a way that some of the original concepts from the original ten proposals would be preserved, which meant that the final proposal inherited some parts from all of the original components in some way.

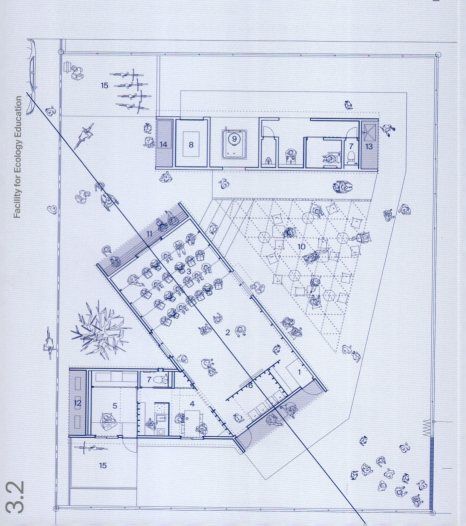

人気が高いものを投票で選ぶと、他の案を支持する人の意見を殺すことになる。投票はあくまで見る人の主体性を引き出す仕掛けであり、結果の大小で多数決を取ることはしない。投票のあとにヒアリングを行い、それぞれの案を支持する人の「選んだ理由」を聞き出す。選んだ理由を知ると、建築のデザインに求めているニーズがわかってくる。

「減額ワークショップ」のあとで、トイレや部屋はできるだけ共有し無駄をなくしていくと同時に、3つの案を支持する理由となる構成要素はすべて残していくように統合した。最終の1案は、3案の評価されたそれぞれの要素がすべて残るように、慎重にデザインされた。3案はオリジナルの10案のオリジナルアイデアの何らかの要素が残るようにデザインされているから、最終1案にはオリジナルの要素が何らか残っている。

これは簡単なようでいて意外と難しい方法論である。かたちを見て特徴を言葉に置き換える練習が必要である。特徴はできるだけ単純な要素としてとらえた方が良い。集団で設計するなら「教会型」「駅舎型」「路地型」と特徴を要約しつつ、

| Plan
平面図
1:200 | 1 Entrance
2 Hall
3 Theater
4 Anteroom
5 Building manager's room
6 Storage
7 Toilet
8 Storage | 9 Water tank space
10 Courtyard
11 Bench
12 Equipment space
13 Exterior handwash basin
14 Bulletin board, vending machine
15 Bicycle parking | 1 玄関
2 ホール
3 表現の舞台
4 控室
5 管理人室
6 収納
7 トイレ
8 倉庫
9 受水槽スペース | 10 中庭
11 ベンチ
12 設備スペース
13 外部手洗
14 掲示板,自動販売機
15 駐輪場 |

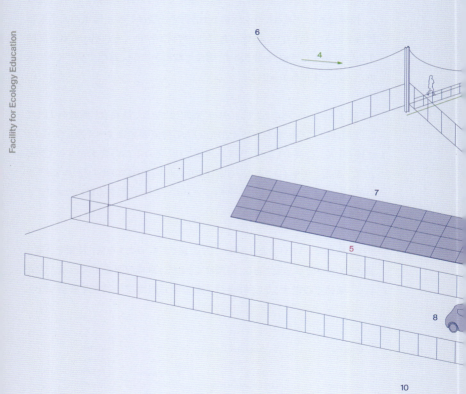

Axonometric drawing アクソメ	1 System, electric power	1 系統, 電力

1 System, electric power
2 Solar power plant, electric power
3 Storage battery electric power
4 Electric poewr supply to the building
* Capable of supplying electric power to the building in case of a disaster
5 Building, EV, Storage battery electric power,
6 From an electric company
7 solar panel (facing south / 10-degree angle)
8 Electric car
9 V2B EV stand + lithium ion batttery V2B
10 Facility for Ecology Education

1 系統, 電力
2 太陽光発電所, 電力
3 蓄電池電力
4 建物へ電力供給
* 災害時停電した際に建物へ電力の供給が可能
5 建物, EV, 蓄電池へ電力供給
6 電力会社より
7 太陽光パネル（真南向き／角度10度）
8 電気自動車
9 V2B EVスタンド＋リチウムイオン電池
10 鶴ヶ島太陽光発電所

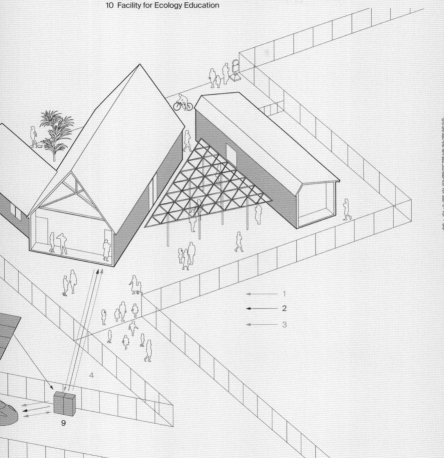

1 Hall	1 ホール
2 Theater	2 表現の舞台
3 Courtyard	3 中庭
4 Bench	4 ベンチ

Facility for Ecology Education

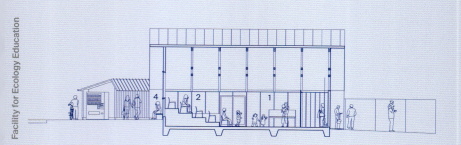

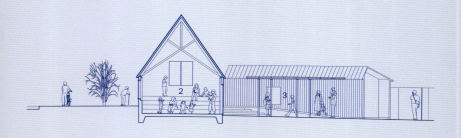

Section │ 断面図 │ 1:250

鶴ヶ島太陽光発電所環境教育施設

3.2

This methodology may sound simple but is actually very difficult to implement, as architects must be properly trained and have the ability to precisely describe formal characteristics in words. It would be better to describe each characteristic in simple words. In my view, a semiotic method of summarizing each characteristic, such as "church type", "station type", and "alley type", was effective in the collective design process, because it successfully evoked people's imagination.

At a symposium at the city hall joined by the mayor and the citizens, Yoshiharu Tsukamoto made an objection to this approach. He stated that, "I find it too crude to label these forms that emerged through the process as a "church", "station", or "alley". There is no church, station or alley in Tsurugashima. We should have a "dialogue with the past" instead of a "dialogue with the future." The mayor objected that it would be difficult to understand this place as an extension of the past, because ties with the history had been broken during the rapid development of the suburban residential area; and we wouldn't be able to create a new place here without taking a highly advanced approach of having a "dialogue with the future."

想像力を喚起する記号的なアプローチがこの設計方法には合っていると感じた。

市役所で市長や市民が同席したシンポジウムでは、このアプローチについて塚本由晴さんから異議が述べられた。塚本さんは「立ち上がってきたかたちに『教会』だとか『駅舎』だとか『路地』だとラベリングすることが暴力的だ。鶴ヶ島には教会も駅舎も路地もない。『未来と対話』するのではなく『過去と対話』するべきだ」という。市長は「歴史を切断して急速に発展した郊外住宅地では過去の延長で場所をとらえることはできない。『未来と対話する』というアクロバティックな回路を採らないとこの場所に場所をつくることはできない」と反論した。

いうまでもなく政治は「今ここ(right here right now)」の判断による影響を強めてしまう。「歴史との対峙」はその後の課題となった。また安易にかたちに「教会」「駅舎」「路地」と名前を与えてしまうことについても、慎重に考える必要があると感じた。

● The facility is used for various activities after the handover.

● 引き渡し後の活動の様子

鶴ヶ島太陽光発電所環境教育施設

206 | 4.0 | Give form to Collective Knowledge

Give form to Collective Knowledge

4.0

4.0 集合的な知にかたちを与える

Aichi Project

is an experiment in publicly designing an imaginary Tokyo Metropolitan Government Office building at an exhibition venue at the international art festival.

—

Although the methodology of collective design we experimented in the Facility of Ecology Education project, namely the "option approach" implemented through public meetings and voting, was a great success, I felt we still had some issues to consider.

—

One of the issues was the number of opinions received during the voting. Even if a workshop is officially announced to invite interested citizens and to hold a vote, the number of people coming to a public meeting would be one hundred at most. When we present several options, we would have to carefully consider the difference between a proposal winning 18 votes and a proposal winning 15 in the evaluation process. Our question was, is it possible to gather more opinions?

—

While I was absorbed in such thoughts, I gained knowledge about the "A/B Test" often used in the field of web design. It is a method of trying both A and B versions and adopt whichever method people preferred, instead of just contemplating which is better. Such approach is feasible in web design thanks to much lower implementation cost than architecture.

—

I was invited to participate in the international art festival Aichi Triennale when I was entertaining such thoughts. Upon learning that each participating artist would be given an exhibition venue in the city center of Nagoya, I conceived an idea of providing a venue where architects openly design an ideal public space.

—

As a precondition, I set an imaginary project of designing "Chukyoto", a new governing body created by integrating Aichi Prefecture and the City of Nagoya. Visitors can see two design proposals on view as well as architects at

4.1 あいちプロジェクト
は、国際芸術祭において
架空の都庁舎を公開で設計する実験である。

「鶴ヶ島太陽光発電所環境教育施設」でパブリックミーティングや投票によるオプション・アプローチによる集団設計の方法論に手応えは感じていたけれど、いくつか課題があると感じていた。

そのうちのひとつは投票などで得られる意見の量である。告知をして関心のある市民を集め、投票を行うとしても、パブリックミーティングに集まるのはせいぜい100名程度。いくつかのオプションを示すと、18票か15票かの違いから差を感じ取る作業が必要になる。もっと多くの意見を集められないか。

そんなことを考えているときに、WEBデザインの世界に「A/Bテスト」なるテストがあることを知った。バージョンAとバージョンBのどちらが優れているか、考えていても仕方がないからとりあえず試してみてより良い反応があった方を採用するというものである。WEBは建築に比べれば実装のコストが格段に低いから、そういうことが可能になる。

「あいちトリエンナーレ」という国際芸術祭への出展を打診されたのは、そんなことを考えていたときだった。出展作家には名古屋市の中心部に会場が用意されるという。それならば、まちの真ん中に理想の公共空間の設計環境をつくってみようと思い立った。

愛知県と名古屋市が統合され「中京都」をつくるという架空のプロジェクトを設定

work at the exhibition venue — making models, attending meetings and so on, and participate in voting at the end. The design team counts votes every day and make new proposals, while carefully studying the vote result and visitors' comments written on the ballots and incorporating them into their design.

In the end, we received more than 4,000 votes during the exhibition period. Quite contrary to the result of the voting participated by one hundred visitors, most opinions turned out to be pretty similar this time. We also spotted some unique opinions from the "minority" voters, which often became a driving force in revising the design from different perspectives.

● The audience were asked to choose one from two given options in the same way as A/B test.

●「A/Bテスト」のように2つのオプションが常に提示され、観客はどちらかを選ぶ

した。展示会場には常に2案が展示され、模型をつくったり打ち合わせをしている風景も見える。来場者は展示されているふたつの案と、ひと通り設計作業の風景を見たあとで、最後に投票することができる。設計チームは期間中毎日開票を行い、票の行方と投票用紙に記入された来場者のコメントを見て次の案を練る。

最終的に会期を通じて4,000票を超える票が集まった。100票くらいの票数の行方とはまったく異なり、ほとんどの意見は似たものになる。なかにマイナーな意見があると光る。デザインを更新していくきっかけになるのはそういうマイナーな意見のほうだった。

	Team H	Team M	Others/その他	Total votes/総得票数
A | 2013.8.10 — 8.24	355	309	70	734
B | 2013.8.24 — 9.8	437	442	85	964
C | 2013.9.8 — 9.21	546	617	107	1270
D | 2013.9.21 — 10.6	693	856	121	1670
Total/合計	2011	2224	383	4618 votes/票

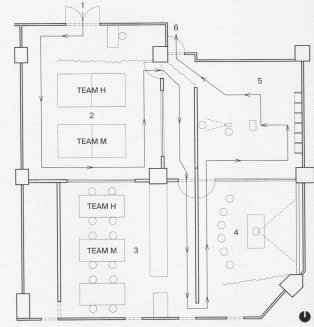

1 Entrance
2 Exhibition Room
3 Model Making Room
4 Movie Room
5 Voting Room
6 Exit

1 入口
2 展示室
3 模型制作室
4 映像室
5 投票室
6 出口

Plan｜会場平面図｜1:100

あいちプロジェクト

4.1

● Vote counting was held on a daily basis. Four thousand votes were collected in total.

● 毎日行われる開票作業。期間中、最終的に4,000を超える票が集まった

Chief Architect
チーフアーキテクト

A | 2013.8.10–8.24

Yosuke Kanematsu
Daiki Yoshii / Mai Ito
Takamichi Irie
Takuya Tanaka

兼松陽介／吉井大貴／伊藤麻衣
入江貴道／田中匠哉

Team H

Yoshiyasu Hirai
平井仁康

● Team H's design process. Their design evolved from the idea of "four corner buildings on the site."

● チームH案の設計プロセス。「4つの角地建築物」というアイデアから発展していった

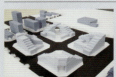

H-001   48 votes/票

H-002   145 votes/票

H-003   83 votes/票

H-004   57 votes/票

H-005   217 votes/票

Team M

Akihiro Murayama
村山明宏

● Team M's design process. Their design evolved from the idea of "a diagonal passage through the site."

● チームM案の設計プロセス。「対角への通り抜け」というアイデアから発展していった

M-001   38 votes/票

M-002   142 votes/票

M-003   60 votes/票

M-004   44 votes/票

M-005   174 votes/票

B | 2013.8.24–9.8

Kohei Miyake / Yuki Katayama
Masato Kato / Sayaka Yoshida
Misaki Syamoto / Kyosuke Fujita
Shuhei Shinkai

三宅航平／片山優樹／加藤正都／吉田紗耶香
社本実咲／藤田恭輔／新海周平

H-006　　　63 votes/票

H-007　　　78 votes/票

H-008　　　79 votes/票

H-009　　　203 votes/票

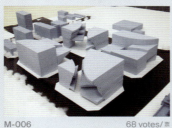
M-006　　　68 votes/票

M-007　　　127 votes/票

M-008　　　73 votes/票

M-008　　　227 votes/票

C | 2013.9.8–9.21

Natsuhiko Zenigame / Misaki Nagaya
Tomoko Ueno / Azumi Eiso / Satomi Suzuki
Shiomi Nagaya / Dai Katsuragawa
銭亀夏彦／長屋美咲／上野友子／永曾あずみ
鈴木里美／長屋汐美／桂川大

H-010 — 242 votes/票
H-011 — 101 votes/票

H-012 — 565 votes/票

M-010 — 287 votes/票
M-011 — 104 votes/票

M-012 — 652 votes/票

D | 2013.9.21–10.6
Yuri Shimizu / Misako Morimoto
清水優里／森本美沙子

H-013　　　　　　　128 votes/票

H-014

M-0103　　　　　　204 votes/票

M-014

展示　>>

チームH プロセス
縮尺 1/2000

チームM プロセス
縮尺 1/2000

223

あいちプロジェクト

4.1

4.2 | G Chair
is an experiment in designing a chair based on images found using image search.

—

While we continued to think of a way in which to design physical objects using more data, we conceived an idea of designing a chair using Google image search. Multiple images of chairs appear under the search keyword "chair" on Google, and I noticed that different images showed up under the keyword "chair" in different languages, such as "いす(*Isu*)" in Japanese, "*Chair*" in English, and "*Silla*" in Spanish.

—

We then used the keyword "chair" in the top nine most spoken languages (Japanese ranks ninth in the world) in Google image search, and classified the chairs appearing in the images into different typologies based on common characteristics in each language. We then extracted top three typologies in each language and integrated them into a single form without eliminating any components constituting each typology, and generated different prototypes using the keyword in different languages, such as "椅子 (yǐzi)" in Chinese, "Chair" in English, and "いす(*Isu*)." The aim of our experiment was to interpret images floating in the internet space as an accumulation of people's memories and to translate specific distribution patterns of chair images in each language space into physical forms.

—

We finally combined these typologies into a single form and conceived a "global" image of a chair shared among people in the world. We decided to call it "Global G Chair."

4.2 | G Chair
は、画像検索によって得られた画像をもとに椅子を設計する試みである。

さらに多くのデータを使って具体物をデザインすることはできないだろうかと考えるうちに、Googleの画像検索を使って椅子をデザインすることを考えた。Googleで「椅子」と画像検索をしてみると、椅子のイメージが表示される。日本語の「いす」と英語の「Chair」、スペイン語の「Silla」では異なる画像が表示されることに気がついた。

そこで世界上位9か国語の（日本語は世界上位9番目の言語である）「椅子」をキーワードに画像検索し、それらの画像に表示された椅子を共通の特徴ごとに類型を抽出する。各国語について3類型を抽出し、それぞれの類型を構成する要素を消去せずにひとつの形態に統合すると、中国語の「椅子」と英語の「Chair」と日本語の「いす」では異なるプロトタイプが生まれた。インターネットに漂う画像を人びとの記憶の束と読み替え、椅子に関する言語空間に固有な分布をかたちにする試みである。

最後にそれらの類型をひとつに統合した。世界の人が思い浮かべる椅子のかたちである。私たちはこれを「Global G Chair」と呼ぶことにした。

G Chair

Arabic | アラビア語

Bengali | ベンガル語

English | 英語
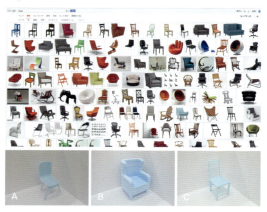

Hindi | ヒンディ語

Portuguese | ポルトガル語
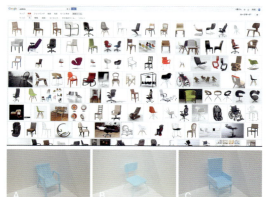

Russian | ロシア語
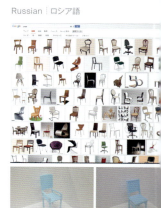

Chinese | 中国語

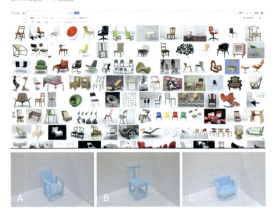

Japanese | 日本語

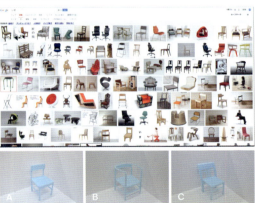

Spanish | スペイン語

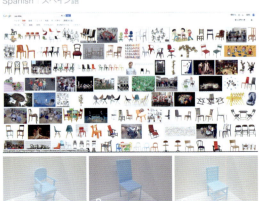

● Images of chairs collected by using Google image search in the nine most spoken languages, and chairs regenerated based on characteristics extracted from the collected images.

● Googleの検索で集められた上位9か国語別の「椅子」の画像とそこから抽出された特徴をもとに再構成された椅子

Chairs integrating top three typologies in each language
各言語3類型を合成した椅子

Arabic｜アラビア語

Bengali｜ベンガル語

Chinese｜中国語

English｜英語

Hindi｜ヒンディ語

Japanese｜日本語

Portuguese｜ポルトガル語

Russian｜ロシア語

Spanish｜スペイン語

● Chairs designed based on images collected by using Google image search in the respective languages.

● Googleの検索で集められた画像をもとにデザインされた各国語の椅子

Universal Language

231

G Chair

● Global G Chair generated by morphing the chairs representing the nine most spoken languages.

● 上位9か国語の椅子を合成して生まれた「Global G Chair」

Design and Fabrication:
Fujimura Laboratory,
Toyo University

設計・制作：
東洋大学藤村研究室

Kyohei Sakamoto
Tatsunobu Tomokuni
Shun Nishimura
Kenta Uchiumi
Sho Takeyama
Masaru Nakano
Ryo Fukui

坂本匡平
友國樹伸
西村峻
内海健太
嶽山渉
中野優
福井遼

4.2

4.3 | G House
is an experiment in designing a house prototype based on images found using image search.

—

After we successfully designed a chair using image search, we proceeded to the next experiment of designing a house using the same method. We did an image search using the keyword "house" to find images and classified them into four house typologies by common characteristics. These typologies were combined into a typical shape of a "house". We conceived a Google-generated house prototype after applying plans, elevations and sections and making some adjustments.

—

I knew that Kazunari Sakamoto (presumably under the influence of Robert Venturi) was doing research on architectural iconography in the 1980's. Sakamoto wrote an essay titled "*Iegata wo Omoi, Motomete* (Contemplating and Pursuing the House-Shape)" in 1979 upon publication of his residential works including *House in Nango, "House in Sakatayamatsuke"* and "*House in Imajuku*", in search of his own "house" shape. As an ardent supporter of Venturi, Sakamoto was well aware of the difference between the architects' concept of a "house" and the general public's conventional image of a "house." While Sakamoto conducted research through questionnaire surveys in the past, we are able to conduct experiments under the same theme using Google search today. The house prototype conceived through the experiment was given the name "G House."

4.3 | G House
は、画像検索によって得られた画像をもとに設計された住宅のプロトタイプである。

画像検索で椅子を設計することができたので、今度は住宅を設計することを試みた。画像検索で「住宅」と検索し、表示された画像を共通する特徴をもとに類型化すると4つの類型が得られた。さらにそれらを統合すると日本中どこにでもあるような典型的な「家」のかたちが取り出された。そこに典型的な平面と立面、断面を与え、整理するとグーグル由来の「家」のプロトタイプが得られた。

1980年代に坂本一成が(おそらくはロバート・ヴェンチューリの影響を受けて)建築の図像性に関する研究をしていたのは知っていた。坂本は1979年に「南湖の家」「坂田山附の家」「今宿の家」の発表に際し、「家形を思い、求めて」というエッセイを発表し、独自の「家」のかたちを追求していた。ヴェンチューリアンである坂本は建築家による概念としての「住宅」と一般人が慣習的に抱く「家」のかたちが異なることに自覚的だった。坂本の研究の手段はアンケート調査だったが、今ではグーグルを用いて近い実験を行うことができる。ここで得られた住宅のプロトタイプを「G House」と名付けた。

A: Single volume, mono-color, gable roof
A：ワンヴォリューム・単色・切妻

A: Integration
A：統合

B: Vertical windows, vertically-laid finishes, shed roof
B：縦長窓・縦の仕上げ・片流れ

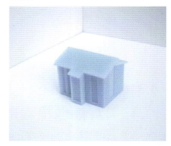

B: Integration
B：統合

C: Different finishes in upper and lower levels, balconies
C：上下の仕上げの切り替え・バルコニー

C: Integration
C：統合

D: Emphasis on horizontality, eaves, setbacks
D：水平強調・庇・セットバック

D: Integration
D：統合

Integration of the four typologies: G House
4つの類型の統合：G House

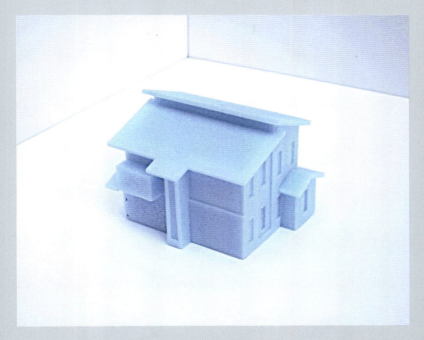

● Images of "houses" collected by using Google image search and houses made by digitally reorganizing characteristics extracted from the collected images.

● Googleの検索で集められた「住宅」の画像とそこから抽出された特徴をもとに再構成された住宅

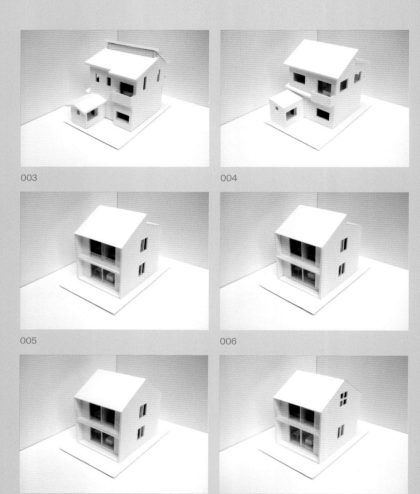

● G House proposed based on houses made by reorganizing the collected "houses" using Google image search.

● Googleの検索で集められた「住宅」から再構成された住宅をもとに提案された「G House」

245

白岡ニュータウンプロジェクト

4.4

4.4 | Shiraoka Newtown Project

are five houses built in a newly developed part of an existing residential district about an hour train ride from central Tokyo.

After releasing a prototype of "G House" along with an estimated construction cost, we were contacted by a developer who wanted to build it. The site was located in a newly developed part of an existing residential district in a suburban new town about an hour train ride from central Tokyo. They were making plans for the last phase of the long residential development that had continued for thirty years and were seeking an effective way to make the best use of the irregularly-shaped site.

The veteran developer has been selling houses in this new town for thirty years and produced a wide variety of houses in different styles based on consumer preferences. This time, he was hoping to reexamine the old method from a fresh perspective because he had no idea what the younger generation wanted.

When you have no idea what to do, the best thing is to design. We first focused on what we were able to decide and translated them into form one by one. We made calculations from the site area and decided to place five blocks of our house prototype on the site. Then we adjusted the sizes and number of rooms and focused more on specific items including the placement of the garden and car parking, entrance approach way and so on. At the end of the process, we conceived a residential district using our prototype and featuring unique gardens that utilize characteristics of the site.

I would like to draw a comparison between "House House" which we carefully studied and designed each of the components including a roof, walls, floors, ceiling, and windows and "Houses in Shirakawa New Town" which we designed using an image search. They are different but also similar in some ways. They both comprise common com-

4.4 | 白岡ニュータウンプロジェクト
は、東京の都心から電車で1時間ほどの 計画住宅地に立つ5棟の販売用の住宅である。

画像検索から得られた「G House」のプロトタイプを工事費の見積り金額とともに発表したところ、「建てたい」というデベロッパーが現れた。敷地は東京の都心から電車で1時間ほどのとあるニュータウンの一角だった。30年にもわたる住宅地開発の最終局面で、変型敷地を有効活用したいということだった。

30年間このニュータウンで住宅を売り続けてきたベテラン担当者は、これまで消費者に寄り添うようにしてさまざまなスタイルの住宅を企画してきたが、今の若い世代は何が好みなのかさっぱりわからない、一度これまでやってきたことを考え直したいという。

「何をやったらいいかわからない」ときこそ、設計するに限る。まずは決めることのできそうなところから少しずつかたちに置き換える。まずは敷地面積から5棟のプロトタイプを並べることとし、その後サイズや部屋数を調整し、庭の配置、駐車場の配置、玄関へのアプローチなど検討項目を増やしていった。プロトタイプを生かしながら、独特の庭で敷地の特徴を生かした住宅地が出来上がった。

建築家として屋根、壁、床、天井、窓などの構成の検討を重ねて設計した「家の家」と、画像検索を用いた「白岡ニュータウンの家」を比べてみると、似ていないといえば似ていないが、似ているといえば似ている。要素がある程度共通しているから、違うといえば構造やディテールの繊細さなどであろうか。それらは私たち建築家にとっては重要な違いだが、他方で要素そのものを劇的に変えなければ新しい建築と認識されないかもしれないと危機感も感じた。

Site plan │ 配置図

● Transition of Shirakawa New Town development. Each house represents a different design of each era.

● 白岡ニュータウンの開発の変遷。時代によって異なる意匠をまとう

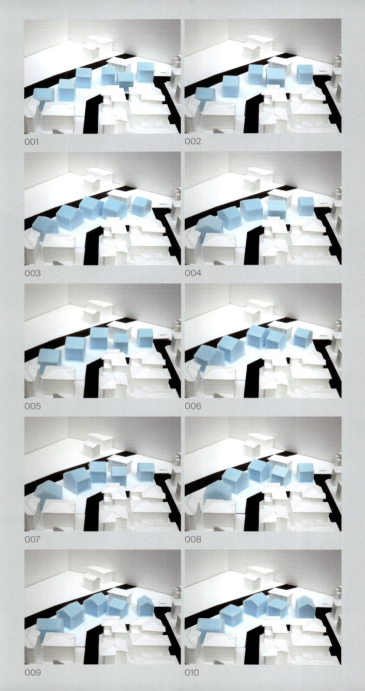

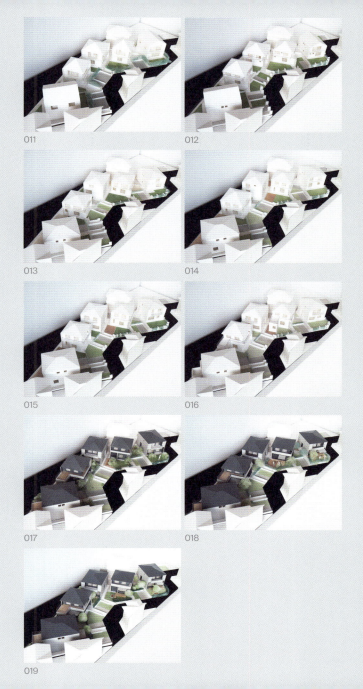

ponents to a certain extent, but are different in terms of the structural systems and details. While such differences are important for architects, they don't influence the general public's perception of architecture. As an architect, I felt an urgency to drastically change the very components constituting architecture in order to create "new architecture" which will be appreciated by the general public.

● Five blocks placed on the site. Various design studies exploring themes such as how to secure a front yard and backyard, the relationship between a garden and a living room, placement of an entrance, and how to connect green zones.

● 並べられた5棟。
前の庭と奥の庭の確保、
庭とリビングの関係、
入口の位置や緑地の連続
などのスタディ

1 Living/dining room	1 リビング・ダイニング
2 Kitchen	2 キッチン
3 Room	3 室
4 Balcony	4 バルコニー

1F plan, 2F plan ｜1F平面図, 2F平面図 ｜1:500

● Wood decks and five gardens in front of houses are interconnected, creating a continuous landscape. Residents can enjoy the view below from terraces where they can put chairs (designed in collaboration with Hajime Ishikawa).

● 住宅の前に設置されたデッキ。
5つの庭が連続してひとつの風景をつくる。
椅子を並べることのできるテラスから
見下ろすことができる（設計協力：石川初）

● Comparison between readymade houses for mass production (left) and houses proposed based on design studies by architects for their clients (right).

●「G House」をもとに
提案された商品化住宅[左]と、
建築家のスタディによって提案された
特定のクライアントのための住宅[右]の比較

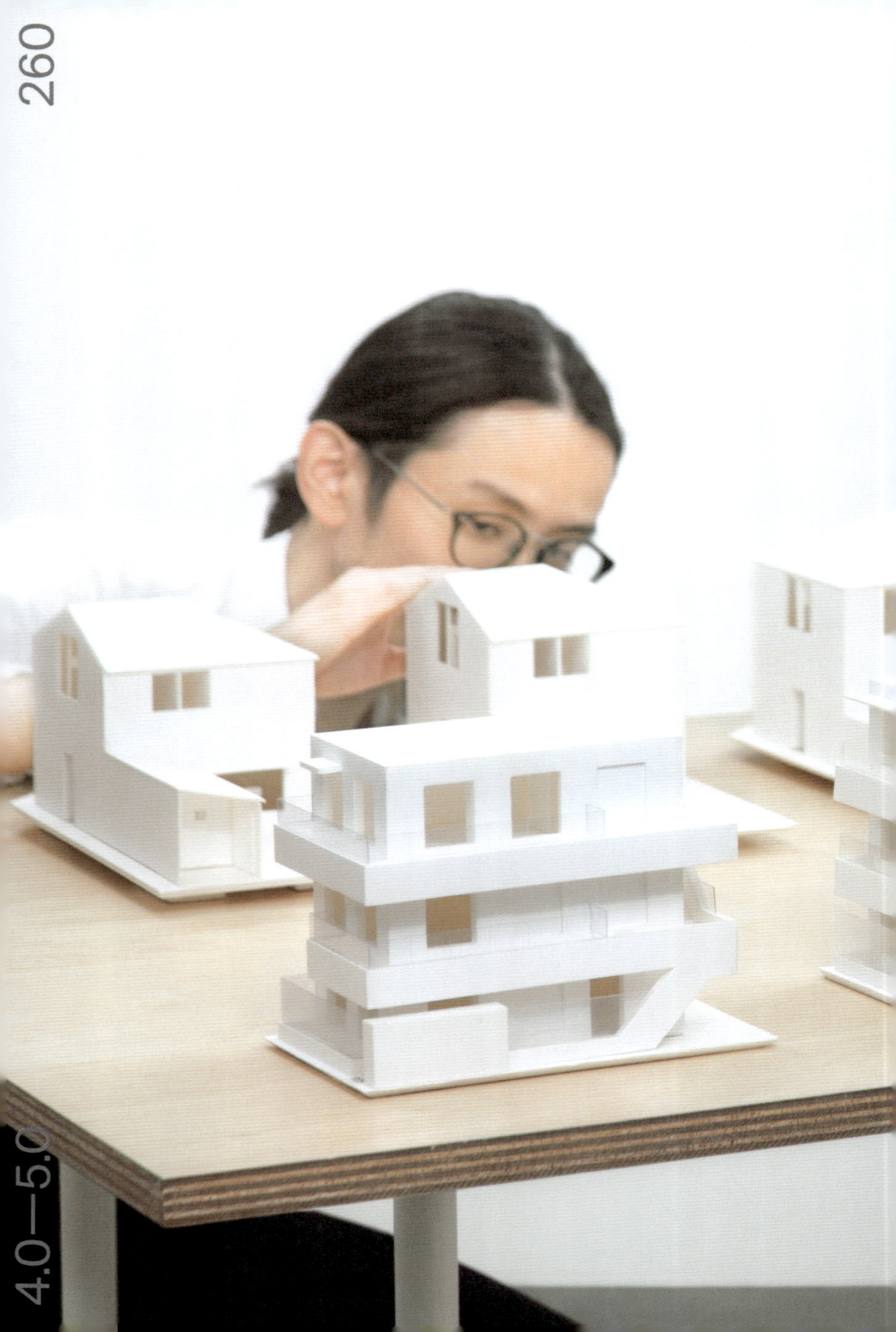

261

4.0—5.0

5.0 From Semiotic to Continuous: Three Experiments with Apartment Building

5.0 記号から連続へ──
3つのアパートの試行錯誤

5.1 APARTMENT S

is an apartment building (containing 9 units) located in a residential area in Tokyo.

In this experiment, our aim was to design a small apartment building without using "symbols" such as a roof, wall, floor, ceiling and window. For a start, we placed a concrete box in the purest form possible and treated openings as "holes" and not as "windows". Our approach may be nothing special because many architects had already taken similar approaches in the past, but it was a very important training for an architect like myself who got accustomed to playing with "symbols."

While closely observing openings punctured at regular intervals on the model, I realized that one of the openings on the first floor faced a garbage storage shed and decided to shift it to avoid the shed. Then we recomposed other openings accordingly in relation to the shifted opening and eventually conceived a unique window layout giving a slightly swaying impression to the building.

Our concept of "treating a box as a box" led to an idea of placing balconies on the north side. Because most people don't hang dry laundry outside in the city center, we made floor plans where each resident opens the door and enters the balcony first before entering the room. This layout allows residents to open windows facing the north balcony and south windows at the same time so that the wind blows through the apartment while keeping the entrance door locked.

In terms of section, we set gradually changing floor heights instead of dividing the building height evenly: the top floor has the lowest ceiling height because it receives the most amount of sunlight, and from the second to fourth floors, the floor height is increased by 50mm than the upper floor so that all floors receive the same amount of light. In this project, we contemplated the meaning of layering in architecture and incorporated benefits [of multistory living] in each room.

5.1　APARTMENT S
は、東京の住宅地に立つ小さな集合住宅(9戸)である。

小さなアパートの設計に際し、屋根、壁、床、天井、窓などの記号を使わないで設計することを試みた。できるだけピュアなコンクリートの箱を用意し、開口を「窓」として設計するのではなく、「穴」として設計する、というように。これまで幾多の建築家が試みてきたことで、特段珍しいことではないかもしれないが、記号の戯れに慣れてしまった自分にとってはとても大事な訓練だった。

均等に空けられた開口をよく眺めると、1階の開口がゴミを保管する倉庫と重なってしまっていることに気がついた。そこでゴミ箱を避けるように開口を動かした。そのことをきっかけにして他の開口との関係が調整され、独特のゆらぎをもつ全体が出来あがっていった。

箱を箱として扱う、という目標がバルコニーを北側に置くというアイデアにつながった。都心部では洗濯物を外に干さないことが多い。そこで階段側の玄関を開けたらいったん外部バルコニーに入り、そこから部屋に入るという平面を設定した。玄関に鍵を掛けていてもバルコニーに向けて建具を開けておけるので南北に風が通り抜ける。

断面に関するアイデアとしては、限られた建物の高さを均等に割るのではなく、階高を50mmずつ変えて、より明るい上の階は高さを絞り、そのぶんより暗くなる下の階に、より多くの高さを配る設定とし、積層することの意味を各部屋に取り込もうとした。

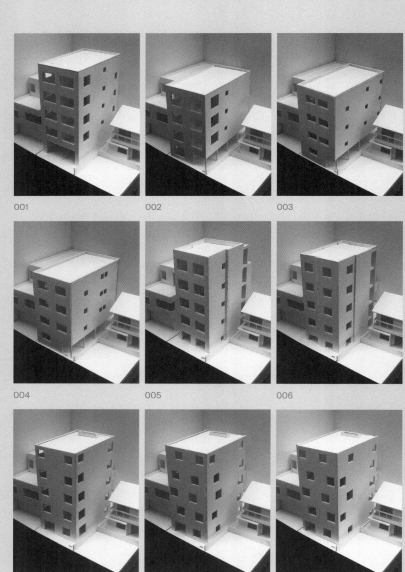

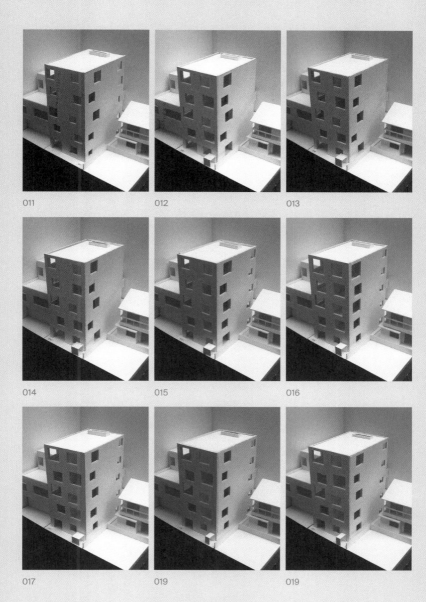

1 Room	1 室
2 Toilet	2 トイレ・脱衣室
3 Bathroom	3 浴室
4 Equipment space	4 設備スペース
5 Common corridor	5 共用廊下

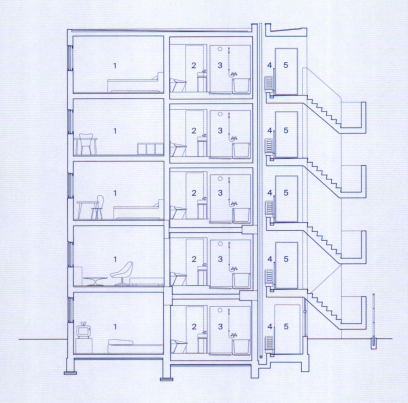

Section | 断面図 | 1:150

● Ceiling heights of the stacked rooms are increased by 50mm per story from bottom to top. Window placement varies in each room.

● 積層された部屋の天井高は50mmずつ変化し、窓の位置はすべての部屋で異なる

501

502

401

402

301

302

201

202

101

エントランス

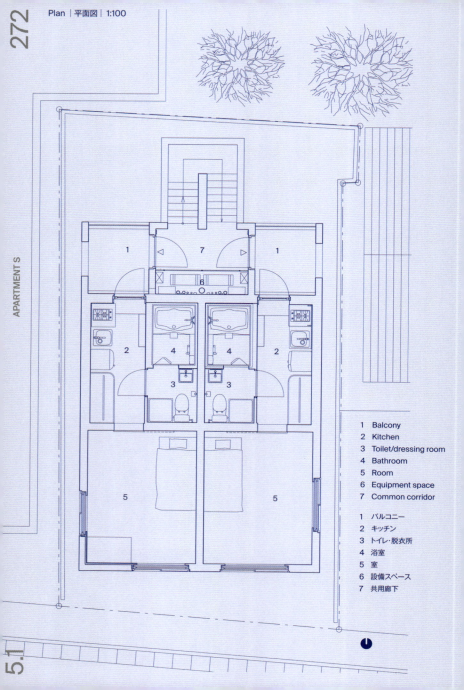

● Inner balconies bring the exterior space into the interior, while directing wind along the north-south axis.

● インナーバルコニーが外部を内部に引き込み、南北通風を可能にする

● No service pipes are exposed on surfaces of the box by concentrating them around the staircase.

● 設備を階段まわりに集約させることで箱の表面には設備が露出しない

5.2 APARTMENT B
is a small apartment building (containing 6 units) located in a residential area in Tokyo.

—

Upon starting the design, we decided to continue the idea of setting a large "box" and puncturing "holes" in this project. In order to emphasize the image of "the box as a box", all baconies are located on the north side and the windows were placed along both vertical sides of the facades. We kept the balcony spandrel walls low at the same height as the window sills (H=400mm above the floor), made the balconies deep enough (W=1200mm) to accommodate furniture, and as a result the proportion of the balconies turned out to be rather oblong. The deep shades of the balconies and the continuous one meter wide concrete strips constituting the spandrel walls create a striking impression on the north facade.

—

Although we succeeded in somehow breaking the conventional proportion of an apartment building, the balconies still look like balconies and the typical contrast between the "box" (main body) and the attached balconies (sub body) still remained. In my view, our next challenge would be to reduce the hierarchy between the main and sub bodies.

5.2 | APARTMENT B
は、東京の住宅地に立つ
小さな集合住宅（6戸）である。

—

引き続き、大きな「箱」に「穴」という仮定で設計を始めた。箱を箱として強調するようにバルコニーを北側に設置し、窓を両端に寄せた。バルコニーの腰壁の高さを窓台の高さ（FL+400mm）に合わせて低くし、家具が置けるように少し出幅を大きく（w=1200mm）すると、バルコニーにしてはプロポーションが横長になった。北側の立面を見ると、バルコニーの陰影が深く、腰壁として現れる幅1mのコンクリートの帯の連続が特徴的である。

—

慣習的なプロポーションは多少崩せたものの、まだバルコニーはバルコニーのかたちのまま残っており、メインの箱とサブのバルコニー、という対比は残っていた。もう少しメインとサブのヒエラルキーをなくしたいと感じた。

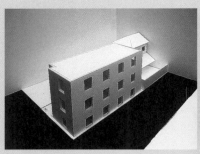
001

002

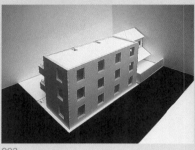
003

004

005

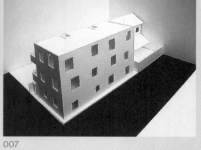
007

008

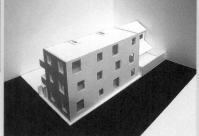
009

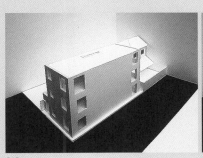
010

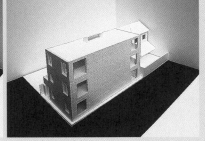
011

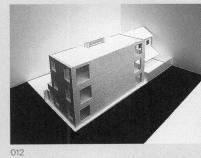
012

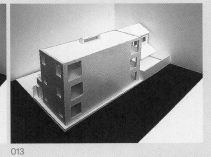
013

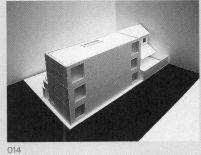
014

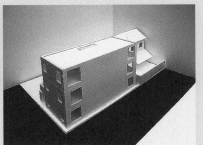
015

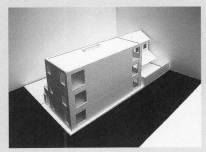
016

● Balconies on the north side are designed slightly deeper than average so that furniture can be placed.

● 北側に通常よりも少しだけ大きな寸法で張り出したバルコニー。家具を出すことができる

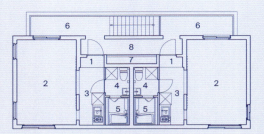

3F plan | 3F 平面図 | 1:200

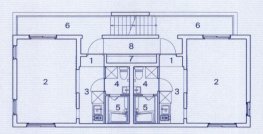

2F plan | 2F 平面図 | 1:200

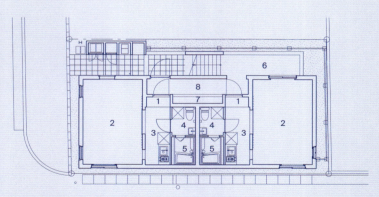

1F plan | 1F 平面図 | 1:200

1	Entrance	1	玄関
2	Room	2	室
3	Kitchen	3	キッチン
4	Toilet/dressing room	4	トイレ・脱衣所
5	Bathroom	5	浴室
6	Balcony	6	バルコニー
7	Equipment space	7	設備スペース
8	Common corridor	8	共用廊下

● No service pipes are exposed on surfaces of the box by concentrating them around the staircase.

● 設備を階段まわりに集約させることで箱の表面には設備が露出しない

5.3 APARTMENT N

is a small apartment building (containing 3 units) located in a residential area in Tokyo.

Meguro, Tokyo, Japan | 2014
pp.288–301

—

Our design initially started from a "box and windows", but I eventually conceived an idea of extending the one-meter wide concrete strips constituting balcony spandrel walls to the entire building. The one meter wide concrete strips functioning as columns and beams constitute a grid structure of the building. The volume is divided in three both in horizontal and vertical directions. The building is very simply composed. The whole body comprises the grid structure made of concrete strips, without the hierarchy of the box (main body) and the attached balconies (sub body) and also without the presence of "symbols" (window).

—

From "BUILDING K" to the series of four houses including "Building HOUSE", "Storage HOUSE", "Shed HOUSE", and "House HOUSE", all I could do was to understand the whole body of architecture as a "mass comprising symbols". After experimenting with the three apartment buildings, I was convinced that we restored the status of architecture from a "semiotic body" to a "continuous body."

5.3 | APARTMENT N
は、東京の住宅地に立つ
小さな集合住宅(3戸)である。

—

当初は箱に窓、というパタンで設計を始めたが、バルコニーの腰壁として現れる幅1mのコンクリートの帯を全体に拡大してはどうかと思い始めた。柱と梁を幅1mのコンクリートの帯のグリッドに吸収させる。断面は上下方向に3分割、平面は奥行方向に3分割。それだけでできている。本体としての箱と付属物としてのバルコニーというヒエラルキーもなく、窓という記号を使わずに、全体を「帯のグリッド」として設計できたと感じた。

—

「BUILDING K」から4つの住宅(「ビルの家」「倉庫の家」「小屋の家」「家の家」)までは建築の全体を記号の塊としてとらえるのに精一杯であった。3つのアパートメントの習作を経て、建築を記号体から連続体へ取り戻せたという感触を得た。

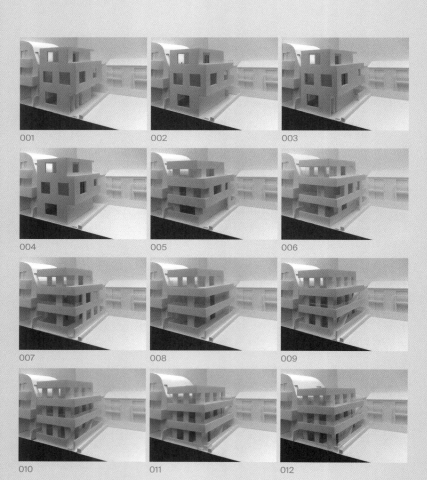

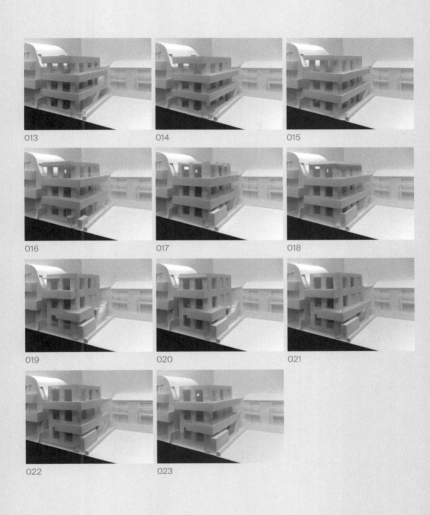

1	Entrance	1	玄関
2	Room	2	室
3	Storage	3	収納
4	Bathroom	4	浴室
5	Balcony	5	バルコニー
6	Equipment space	6	設備スペース

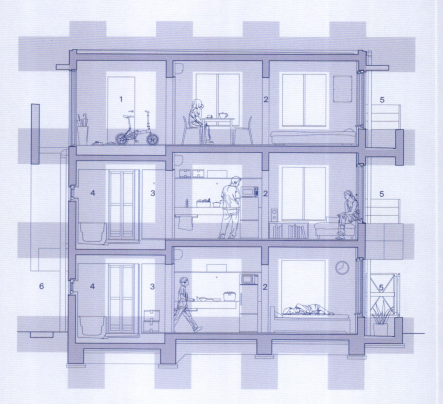

Section｜断面図｜1:100

● 1m-wide concrete strips create a grid system constituting the whole. The structure is equally divided in three in vertical and horizontal directions.

● 1m幅のコンクリートの帯がグリッドをなして全体を構成する。高さ方向奥行方向にそれぞれ3等分割

1 Entrance
2 Room
3 Storage
4 Dressing room
5 Bathroom
6 Toilet
7 Balcony
8 Equipment room

1 玄関
2 室
3 収納
4 脱衣所
5 浴室
6 トイレ
7 バルコニー
8 設備スペース

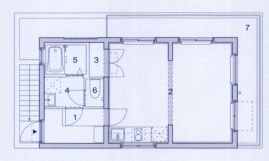

3F plan | 3F 平面図 | 1:150

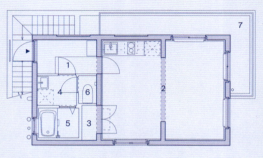

2F plan | 2F 平面図 | 1:150

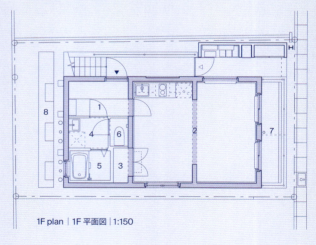

1F plan | 1F 平面図 | 1:150

● Wall-columns loosely divides between the bedroom and dining room.

● 壁柱がベッドルームとダイニングを緩やかに分ける

APARTMENT S   APARTMENT B

● Three apartments.
From a box to strips,
from semiotic to continuous.

● 3つのアパート。
箱から帯へ、記号から連続へ

APARTMENT S

APARTMENT B

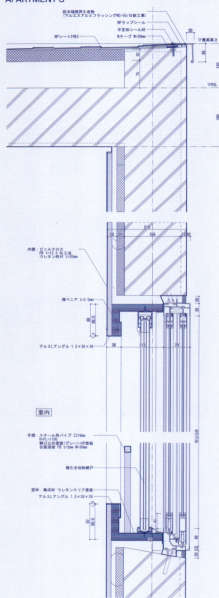

Comparison of window detail drawings
窓まわり詳細図の比較

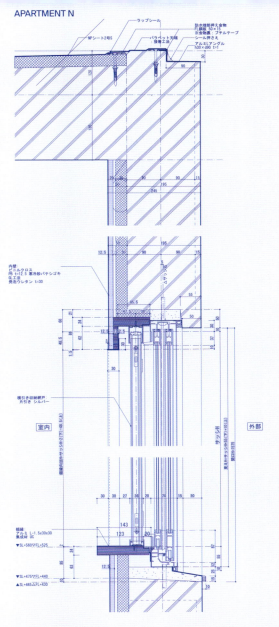

● Section details of the three apartments. Details including waterproofing, window sash and frames have evolved based on lessons learned.

● 3つのアパートの断面詳細。防水、サッシ、枠まわりの収め方は学びながら進化していった

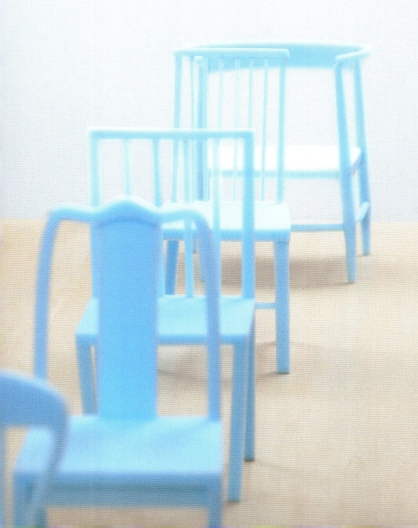

308 | 6.0 | Towards Collective and Continuous Architecture

6.0

6.0　集合的かつ連続的な建築へ

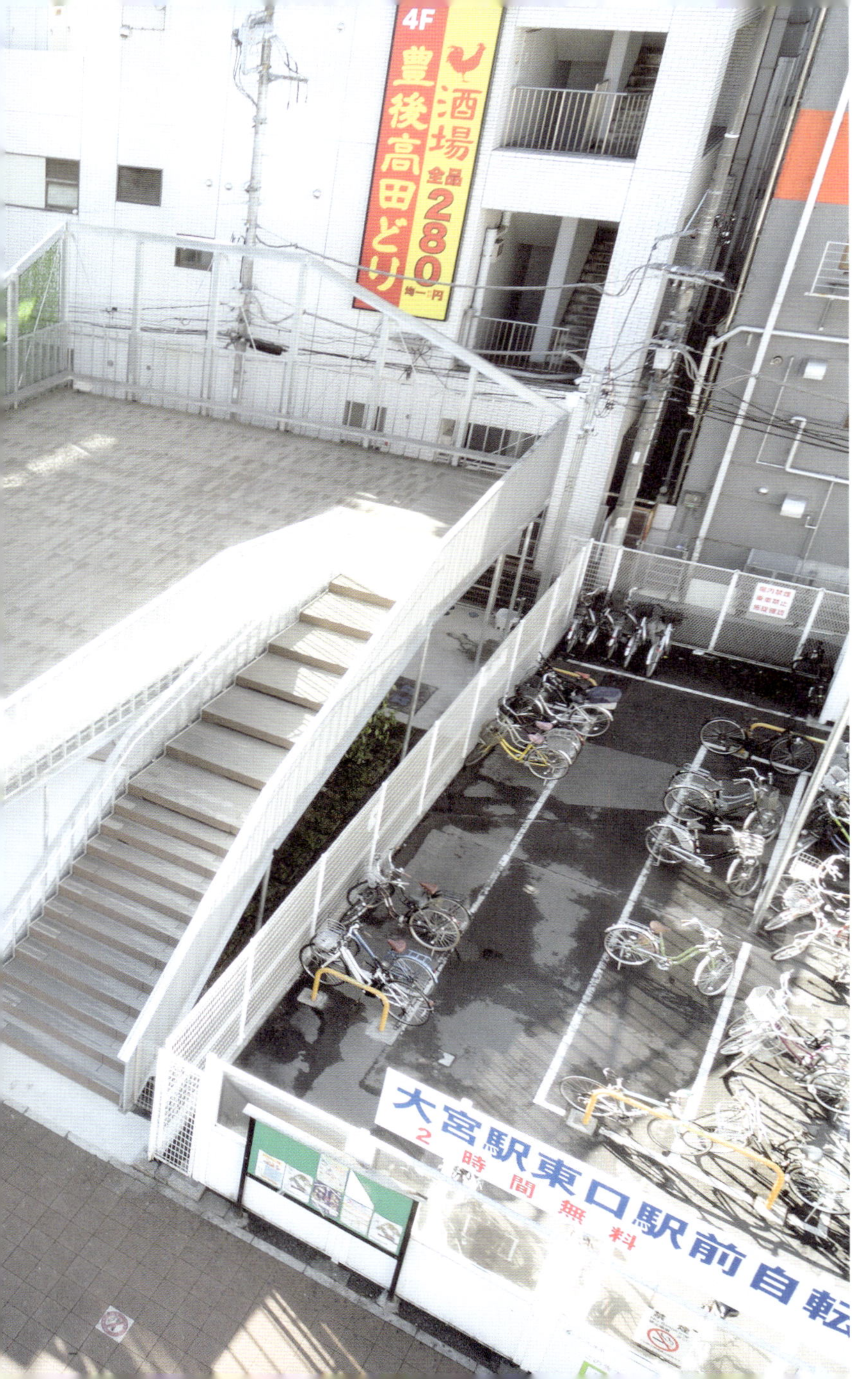
4F
酒場
全品
280
豊後高田どり
大宮駅東口駅前自転
2時間無料

6.1 | OM TERRACE

is a small public facility located in front of a train station in the suburb of Tokyo, comprising a public toilet, rental cycle port and rooftop square.

Saitama City, in response to the citizens' long-time demand, made a plan to rebuild a public toilet on a municipally owned land in front of Omiya Station. One of the project aims was to strengthen "omotenashi" (hospitality) functions in anticipation of international events including the 2020 Tokyo Olympics/Paralympics games to be held in Omiya. I was selected by the city as the architect and also requested us to work with local residents to decide what "omotenashi" functions the city should offer to visitors.

According to a questionnaire survey, many citizens requested clean public toilet and free Wi-Fi connection. On the other hand, we had vigorous discussions with local business owners at public meetings. Omiya is a key transport hub and the real estate value is high. They were concerned that the majority of businesses are nationwide chain stores due to high rents and that there are few new local businesses, and suggested that this land should be utilized for development of local entrepreneurship. I was convinced that what we needed to do was to open the streets, squares and parks to the public and promote development of new players in local businesses, and create architecture that resonates with activities in these public spaces.

Our design aimed to wisely use the budget secured for the public toilet and realize the entire building as a continuous body like a street. The public toilet and bicycle port on the first floor and the rooftop terrace were connected by two

6.1 | OM TERRACE
は、東京郊外の駅前に建つ、トイレとレンタサイクルのポート、屋上広場からなる小さな公共施設である。

―

さいたま市の大宮駅前に市が所有する土地があり、従前から要望のあった公衆トイレを建て替えようという話が出た。その際、大宮では東京オリンピック・パラリンピックなどの国際イベントが開催されることから「おもてなし機能」を強化するという目標が立てられた。具体的に何をもって「おもてなし」とするかは地元と対話しながら定めてほしいという条件のもと、私は設計者として選ばれた。

―

アンケートではきれいなトイレを望む声が多く、Wi-Fiが欲しいという声も聴かれた。他方でパブリックミーティングではまちの商業との関連で意見が多く交わされた。交通結節点である大宮は不動産価値は高いものの、賃料が高いためにナショナルチェーンの店舗が多く、新しい商業事業者が育っていない。だから、この土地は、事業者の育成のために使うべきだというものだった。道路や広場公園などの公共空間を積極的に開放することで新しい商業プレイヤーを育て、まちを活性化する。そのことがまちの「おもてなし機能」を高める。そんな今日のパブリックスペースの考え方に呼応する建築をつくりたいと考えた。

―

トイレのために確保された予算をやりくりして、全体を「ストリートのようなひとつながりの連続体」として実現したいと考えた。1階のトイレや駐輪場、屋上のテ

sets of gently inclined stairs where the gradient changes half way. The handrails and walls placed around the public toilet and on the stairs and roof terrace were designed as continuous elements where materials switch from one to another according to required functions, such as allowing vision through the wall, blocking vision, serving as surface to mount a screen and so on. Sections of steel members constituting the main structure (the primary members, or the "1st" members in Japanese) were designed as slender and light as possible, while sections of members constituting handrails where benches and counters are attached (the secondary members or the "2nd" members") were made rather bulky considering the weight of benches and also the wind load against the screen. It is as if constructing the entire building of "1.5th" members. This method became one of the ways to deal with various requests in designing "architecture as a continuous body."

The bottom-up design process conducted in conjunction with the urban planning process may be an effective means for the realization of architecture liberated from the rigidity of systematic and rational architecture idealized in Modernism and to flexibly respond to various needs. While Incrementalism initially took a critical view of the failure of modernism, we cannot negate the possibility that Incrementalism may fall into routines of ad hoc measures which would result in the same type of Modernist rigidity. With this project, I hope to present a new definition of "continuous body" in order to push forward the bottom-up approach on an urban site.

The concept of "continuous body", exemplified in projects including "Jussieu – Two Libraries" (OMA) and "Yokohama International Passenger Terminal" (foa) and discussed from the 1990's to the 2000's, was conceived under the influence of the social trend toward "continuity" after the world witnessed the historic moments of the fall of the Berlin Wall and the European integration. Today, the concept of "continuity" sends us a strong message in the era of ever-accelerating division as exemplified by Brexit and the inauguration of Trump administration.

ラスを緩く変化のあるふたつの階段でつなげる。トイレから階段、テラスにかけて設置する手すりや壁を、場所によって透過させたい、目隠ししたい、スクリーンを取り付けたい、などの要求条件の違いを反映して素材を切り替えつつ連続的に変化させる。また主要構造部を構成する鉄骨の1次部材は断面を限りなく軽快なサイズとし、ベンチやカウンターの設置される手すりを構成する2次部材はベンチの荷重やスクリーンの風荷重を負担させるため部材の断面を少し大きなものとし、全体が「1.5次部材」で構成されたかのようにして扱う。「連続体としての建築」が、多様な要求と向き合うひとつの構えとなった。

—

まちづくりの過程に寄り添い、ボトムアップで設計していくことは、計画的で合理的な建築を目指す近代主義が次第に陥ったような硬直性を回避し、ニーズにより柔軟に応えることを実現するかもしれない。しかしそのような近代主義の反省に立ったはずの漸進主義は、やがて場当たり的な対応に陥って、新たな硬直を生む可能性は否定できない。まちづくりの現場でボトムアップの姿勢を貫くためにも、新しい「連続体」の解釈を示していきたいと考えている。

—

「パリ大学ジュシュー校図書館コンペ案」(設計：OMA, 1992) や「横浜港大さん橋国際客船ターミナル」(設計：foa, 2002) などを通じて1990年代から2000年代にかけて議論された「連続体」というコンセプトは、ベルリンの壁の崩壊やEU統合による新しい「連続」の機運のなかで生み出されたが、英国離脱やトランプ政権発足という「分断」が加速する現代にこそ、「連続」はメッセージ性を帯びる。

● Examples of continuous architecture. "Jussieu – Two Libraries" by OMA (1992) and "Yokohama International Port Terminal" by foa (2002).

● OMA「パリ大学ジュシュー校図書館コンペ案」(1992) と foa「横浜港大さん橋国際客船ターミナル」(2002) の連続体

318

The 1st public meeting	The 2nd public meeting	The 3rd public meeting
第1回パブリックミーティング	第2回パブリックミーティング	第3回パブリックミーティング
2016.2.5	2016.3.15	2016.3.25

OM TERRACE

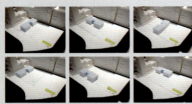

Building placement study｜配置検討

Separate volume scheme｜分棟案

Triangle scheme｜三角案

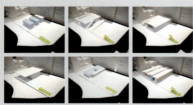

Large roof scheme｜大屋根案

Mall scheme
モール案

Inviting garden + pointed roof scheme
引き込み庭＋とんがり屋根案

Large stairway scheme
大階段案

Roof scheme
屋上案

Cloister scheme
回廊案

Courtyard scheme
大屋根案

6.1

PM1

PM2

PM3

The 4th public meeting
第4回パブリックミーティング
2016.4.22

The 5th public meeting
第5回パブリックミーティング
2016.9.5

The 6th public meeting
第6回パブリックミーティング
2017.2.28

319

Roof scheme
屋上案

Cloister scheme
回廊案

Final scheme | 最終案

OM TERRACE

Courtyard scheme
大屋根案

● The process of developing a continuous body through six public meetings.

● 6回のパブリックミーティングの積み重ねから連続体を見出していくプロセス

PM4　　　　　　　　　　PM5　　　　　　　　　　　　　PM6

6.1

● The first-floor space accommodates all required functions. We proposed a passage traversing the site and a bench even though they were not initially request, because we were concerned that the backstreet should be made brighter from an urban design point of view.

● 求められた機能を配列した1階の空間。通り抜けや半透明の壁やベンチは求められていなかったが、奥の裏道を明るくするという都市デザイン上の配慮から提案した

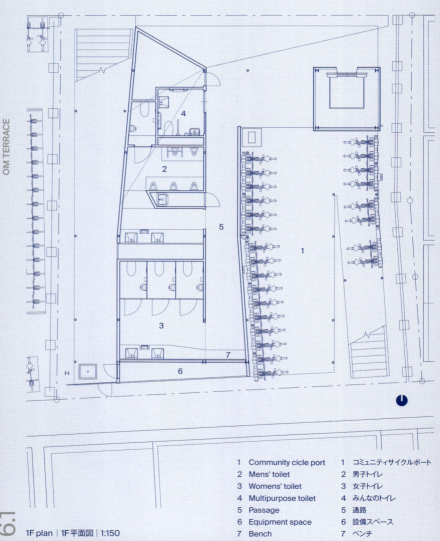

1	Community cicle port	1	コミュニティサイクルポート
2	Mens' toilet	2	男子トイレ
3	Womens' toilet	3	女子トイレ
4	Multipurpose toilet	4	みんなのトイレ
5	Passage	5	通路
6	Equipment space	6	設備スペース
7	Bench	7	ベンチ

1F plan | 1F平面図 | 1:150

322

1 Terrace
1 テラス

● We proposed a raised square where people can look around the city on the second floor, even though it was not initially requested.

● 当初求められていなかったが提案された2階の空間。街を眺めることのできる、もち上げられた広場

OM TERRACE

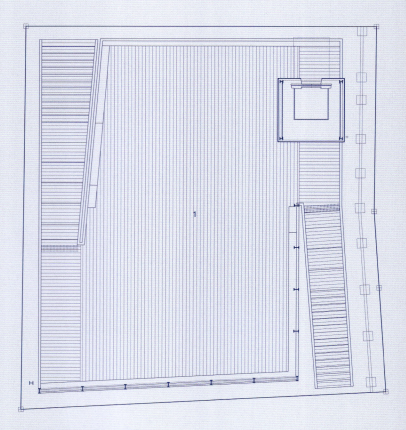

Roof plan │ 屋上 平面図 │ 1:150

6.1

OM TERRACE

324

● Continuous circulation without dead ends. Architecture where one can continuously circulate around the space.

● 行き止まりがなく、連続的な動線。ぐるぐると回遊することができる建築

OM TERRACE

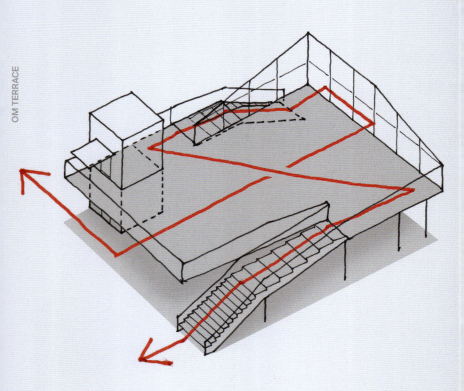

6.1

OM TERRACE

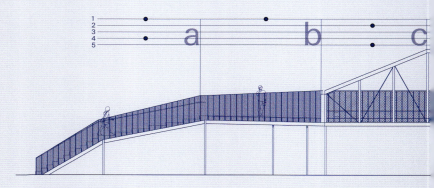

Handrail detail drawing | 手すり展開図 | 1:200

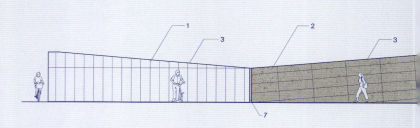

Wall detail drawing | 壁展開図 | 1:200

● The continuous wall is finished with different materials according to the requirement of each space.

● 素材を場所ごとの要求に従って張り分けながら連続する壁

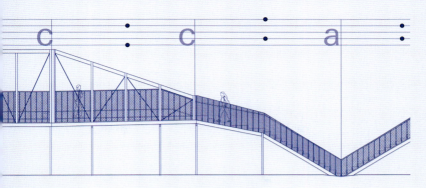

1	Perforated aluminum panel	1	アルミパンチングメタル
2	Diamond wire mesh	2	菱形金網
3	Tempered glass	3	強化ガラス
4	Staircase	4	階段
5	Bench/counter	5	ベンチ・カウンター

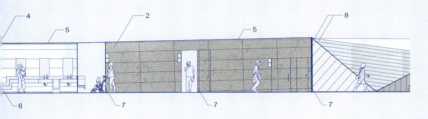

1	Flexible board t=6 AEP@500	1	フレキシブルボード t=6 AEP@500
2	High pressure wood wood cement board t=15 AEP horizontal installation	2	高圧木毛セメント板 t=15 AEP 横張り
3	Aluminum parapet cap t=5	3	アルミ笠木 t=5
4	Lume wall t=40 horizontal installation	4	ルメウォール t=40 横張り
5	Parapet cap lighting	5	笠木照明
6	Polished terrazo t=10	6	人造石研出し t=10
7	Stainless steel mirror finish	7	SUS鏡面
8	Aluminum spandrel t=1 2@300	8	アルミスパンドレル t=12@300

1	Handrail cap: StFB-9×100 Galvanized steel	1	手すり笠木：StFB-9×100 溶融亜鉛メッキ
	Handrail cap: StFB-16×65@300 Galvanized steel		手すり支柱：StFB-16×65@300 溶融亜鉛メッキ
2	Supplementary handrail ○-34×1.2 Galvanized steel	2	補助手すり：○-34×1.2 溶融亜鉛メッキ
3	Handrail panel: perforated metal t=2 Φ5×10.0P	3	手すり面材：パンチングメタル t=2 Φ5×10.0P
4	Handrail panel: diamond wire mesh Φ2.6×32	4	手すり面材：菱形金網 Φ2.6×32
5	Bench: artificial wood deck t=25	5	ベンチ：人口ウッドデッキ t=25
	Supporting beam: SS FB16×65		支持梁：SS FB16×65
6	LED lighting	6	LED照明
7	Floor: artificial wood deck t=25	7	床：人口木ウッドデッキ t=25
8	Handrail panel upper and lower frames: L-14.7×30×2.3	8	手すり面材上枠・下枠：L-14.7×30×2.3
9	Stair: artificial wood deck t=25	9	階段：人口ウッドデッキ t=25
10	Counter: artificial wood deck t=25,	10	カウンター：人口ウッドデッキ t=25,
	supporting beam: StFB-25×50		支持梁：StFB-25×50
11	frame for glass: StFB-30×30×1.6	11	ガラス枠：StFB-30×30×1, 手すり面材：強化ガラス t=6×2, 飛散防止フィルム（内）, 目隠し用フィルム（外）
	handrail panel: tempered glass with shatterproof film (inside) and privacy film (outside)		

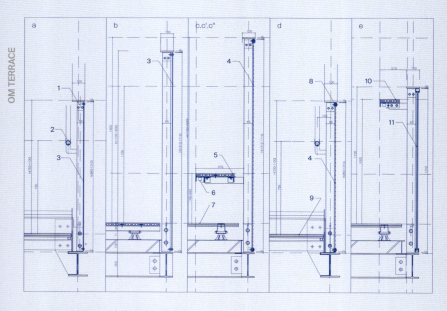

Handrail detail drawing｜手すり詳細図｜1:30

● The primary (or the 1st) components (including the main structural elements such as floors) are designed as thin as possible and the secondary (or the 2nd) components (including handrails) are designed as thick as possible, based on our idea that all components should be treated as the "1.5th components." Components including the stairs and benches are attached to both sides of the handrails at designated locations.

● 床など主要構造部をつくる1次部材を細く、手すりなどをつくる2次部材を厚く、全体を「1.5次部材」として扱う。手すりの左右に階段やベンチなど、場所ごとに必要な部材が取り付く

● Furniture floating in front of the light wall continuously transforms from a wash counter to a bench.

● 光る壁に浮かんだ、洗面カウンターからベンチへと連続的に変化する家具

335

つるがしま中央交流センター

6.2

6.2 | Tsurugashima Central Community Center

is a reconstruction project of a community assembly hall reprogrammed as an operation hub for local businesses and incorporating new functions.

Our aim was to design the entire building based on the concept of "continuous body", a theme succeeded from the OM TERRACE project. The program included several functions including an assembly room, community restaurant, office and community general support center. I conceived an idea of making horizontal ribbon windows traversing the entire space and connecting all functions — envisioned as windows open to the community to show the presence of this facility.

While the assembly room required a high ceiling space, we wanted to keep the building height along the road where cherry trees grow. In addition, the metal corrugated roof required a water gradient of 3/100. The roof is split in two and set at the highest point above the assembly room requiring the highest ceiling, which inclines towards the road and folds back to reach the lowest point above the toilet on the north side. The roof structure comprises two rows of repetitive gate-like frames.

I was tempted to use a simple form like the Faculty of Ecology Education, but refrained from doing so and patiently continued the dialogue with the community residents. Even though it would have been much easier to think of the building as a "symbol", we continued to make proposals based on the required functions, while comparing floor plans. In retrospect, it took a lot of patience to complete this project.

6.2 つるがしま中央交流センター
は、住民のための集会所に新たな機能を加え、地域の経営拠点として建て替えるプロジェクトである。

「OM TERRACE」に引き続いて「連続体」というモチーフで全体を設計しようと考えた。集会室、コミュニティ・レストラン、オフィス、地域包括支援センターなど、いくつかの機能があった。それらを横断するように水平の連窓でつなぐことを考えた。地域に開き、施設の存在を伝えるための水平連窓である。

集会室は高さが求められたが桜の木がある道路側はできるだけ低く構えたい。また金属折板屋根は3/100の水勾配を取ることを求められた。そこで屋根は高さの求められる集会室部分からスタートして、道路側で折り返して北側のトイレ部分が一番低くなるように架けることとした。構造的には鳥居のような門型のフレームが反復して2列並んだような建築である。

「鶴ヶ島太陽光発電所環境教育施設」のようにわかりやすい形態にしてしまいたい誘惑にかられた。でもそれをしないで粘り強く対話を続けた。シンボルにしてしまえば楽なのに、平面図を比べながら、求められる機能と提案を続けた。辛抱強さが必要なプロジェクトだった。

- Hall
- Multipurpose meeting room
- Salon
- Community kitchen
- Central mutual support council office
- Storage
- Community support center

2017.4.8 | Proposals for consideration | 検討案

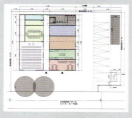

2017.4.8 | Proposals for consideration | 検討案

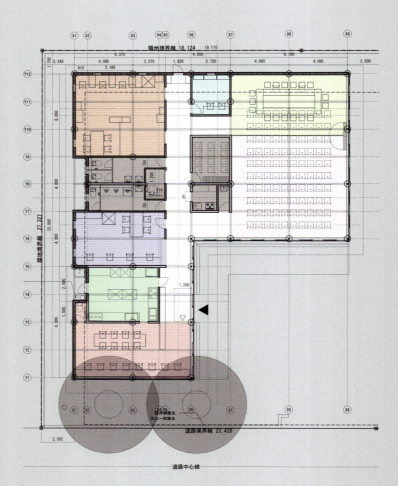

● The plan was completed after a series of dialogues with the community. The "community kitchen" to be shared among the community is placed on the south side at the most visible location.

● 対話を経て完成した平面図。キッチンを「コミュニティキッチン」として機能するように南側の一番目立つところへ配置した

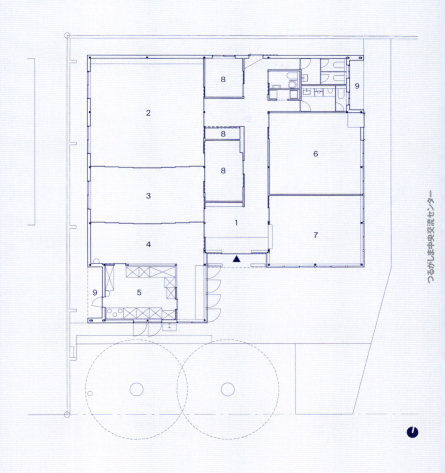

1	Entrance hall	1	玄関ホール
2	Hall	2	広間
3	Multipurpose meeting room	3	多目的会議室
4	Salon	4	交流サロン
5	Community kitchen	5	コミュニティキッチン
6	Community support center	6	地域包括支援センター
7	Central mutual support council office	7	中央支え合い協議会事務所
8	Storage	8	倉庫
9	Equipment space	9	設備スペース

Plan | 平面図 | 1:250

● Horizontal ribbon windows are opened across different functions, introducing activities inside to the city.

● 異なる機能を横断するように開けられた、水平に連続する窓。内部の活動をまちへ開く

● The roof is divided in two sections inclined at the same angle. An assembly room is placed under the highest point and utility rooms are placed under the lowest point of the roof. The two sections meet at the low roof line parallel to the road.

● ひとつの勾配が2枚の屋根にわけられて連続する。最も高いところに集会室、最も低いところに水まわり、道路に面したところの高さは低く抑えられて揃う

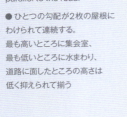

List of components｜部材リスト

Pillars｜柱
■-100×100
□-100×100×9 or 12
□-200×100×9

Truss Beams｜トラス梁
Beams｜梁：75×45×3.2
Trusses｜束：□-100×200×9

Beams｜梁
H-200×100×5.5×8
Box H-200×100×5.5×8
StPl-t=3.2

Braces｜ブレース
M16

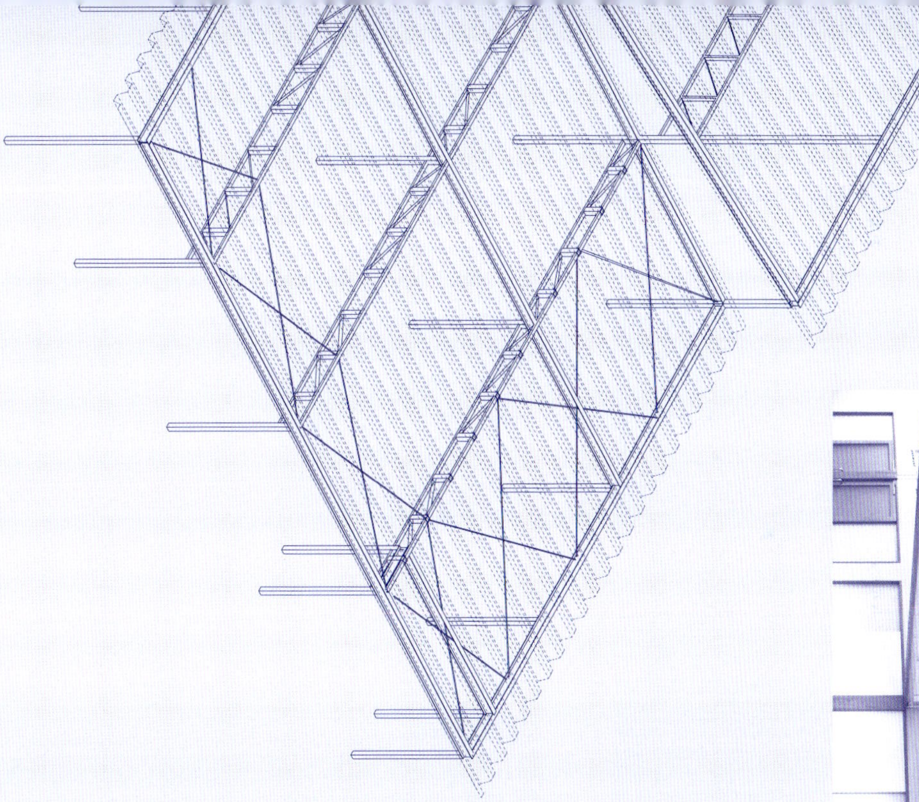

347

6.2　つるがしま中央交流センター

1 Hall
2 Multipurpose meeting room
3 Salon
4 Community kitchen

1 広間
2 多目的会議室
3 交流サロン
4 コミュニティキッチン

● Different functions are placed side by side in an expansive space under the inclined roof.

● 傾いた屋根の下に異なる機能をもった空間が等価に並べられる

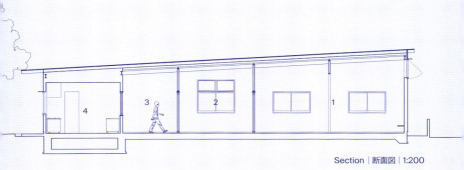

Section｜断面図｜1:200

● A view from the assembly room to the salon and community kitchen. The hanging walls are structural components which also serve as transparent partition walls. They are intended to emphasize the continuity of the roof.

● 集会室から交流サロン、コミュニティキッチンを望む。垂れ壁は構造でもあり、透明な間仕切りの一部として屋根の連続性を強調する

356 | 7.0 | Architecture as the "Form of Knowledge"

7.0

7.0 「ちのかたち」としての建築

すばる保育園

7.1 | Subaru Nursery School
is a nursery school relocated from a different location and built on a site in the suburb of Fukuoka.

The client requested us to design a durable building where children are securely protected after experiencing the 2016 Kumamoto Earthquakes which occured right before this project started. The nursery school also emphasizes physical education and requested us to divide the building in two nursery rooms to accommodate two age groups, namely a group of younger children (0, 1, and 2 years old) and a group of older children (3, 4 and 5 years old), to facilitate children's physical activities according to the level of their physical growth.

When we visited the site, there was an adjoining sacred grove of a local shrine on the west side, and one can enjoy a panoramic view of the vast expanse of rice fields with Hanatate Mountain and the continuous mountain range in the distance towards the northeast direction. I felt that we needed to carefully consider how to connect these surroundings with the nursery school building.

We provided two gardens adjoining each nursery room — one facing the sacred grove and the other facing the rice fields on the south side. The sinuous building meanders around each garden, and administrative rooms including a teachers' room are placed at "nodes" where one can watch over children's activities. In addition, an assemby hall with a raised stage is located at the corner, constituting an irregular S-shaped floor plan.

We studied few possible options regarding the roof structure. We needed to pay attention to various requested conditions in each place: the eaves must be 2 meters deep to shield the building from heavy rain and strong wind in case of typhoon, and the required ceiling height above the stage in the assembly hall had to be more than 4 meters. In the end, we conceived a continuous envelope comprising 180

7.1 すばる保育園
は、福岡の郊外に
移転新築された保育園である。

クライアントはプロジェクトが始まる直前に起きた熊本での震災を経て、子どもたちを守りたいとの思いから強さのある建築を希望された。またこの保育園では体育教育に力を入れており、3歳未満児(0、1、2歳)と3歳以上児(3、4、5歳)では身体の発達に大きく差があることから、園舎を大きく2つの部分に分けることが求められた。

敷地を訪れると西隣には神社の鎮守の森が隣接しており、北東方向には水田が広がると同時に遠く花立山(はなたてやま)とそれに連なる山並みを望むことができた。これらの周辺環境と園舎をいかに関係付けるかを考慮する必要があると考えた。

それぞれの保育室用にふたつの園庭をつくり、ひとつは鎮守の森に、もうひとつは南側の水田に向け、それぞれの園庭を囲うように園舎を大きくカーブさせ配置した。室内外の子どもたちの動きを見渡せる結節点に職員室を含めた管理

mm thick concrete slabs where the walls seamlessly turn into eaves and gently rising three-dimensionally curved roof. The three-dimensionally curved surface of the roof was decided through design optimization analysis aiming to minimize the structural strain, which spans the 15 meter wide 4 meter high space with no columns and which merges with the walls to constitute an integrated structure.

From inside the hall, the view of the mountains in the distance, framed by the horizontal ribbon windows, appears very close. When seen from the outside, the undulating roof shape generated using a machine language of algorithmic design and the shape of Hanatate Mountain formed by the force of nature overlap each other to create a continuous scenery where the architecture merges into the surrounding landscape. I was convinced that we successfully realized the idea of "architecture as a continuous body" that becomes one with abundant nature.

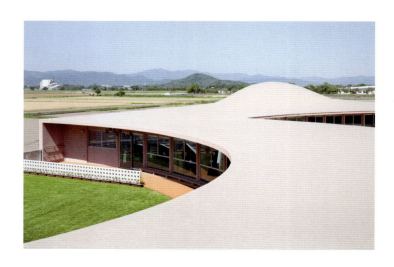

諸室を、角にステージの付いたホールを配置すると、結果的に変則的なS字のカーブの平面となった。

—

屋根の構造についてはいくつかの可能性を検討した。台風時の雨の吹き込みを考慮して軒を2m出すこと、音楽の演奏や屋内での運動に用いるホール部分はステージ上で高さ4mの高さを確保することなど、場所ごとに異なる要求があった。最終的に鉄筋コンクリートの平板が同じ180mmの厚さで軒先から園舎の屋根へ連続し、そのまま3次元曲面によってスラブが隆起することでホールの屋根とする連続的な形式となった。自由曲面屋根の形態は、ひずみエネルギー最小化を目的とする最適化設計により形態が決定され、天井高4m、横15mのスパンの空間を無柱・無梁で覆い、壁と屋根を一体の構造とすることができた。

—

ホールの内側から見ると水平に切り取られた連窓からは遠景の山並みを近くに感じることができる。外側から見ると盛り上がった屋根の形状と、遠くに見える花立山の形状が重なって見え、アルゴリズミック・デザインによる機械言語による形態と、自然の形態がぴったりと重なり、連続した風景となっている。子どもの成長に寄り添い、豊かな自然環境と一体となる「連続体としての建築」が実現できたと感じた。

園舎全景より

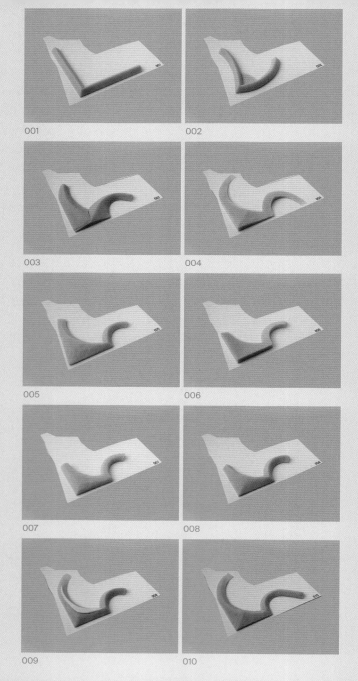

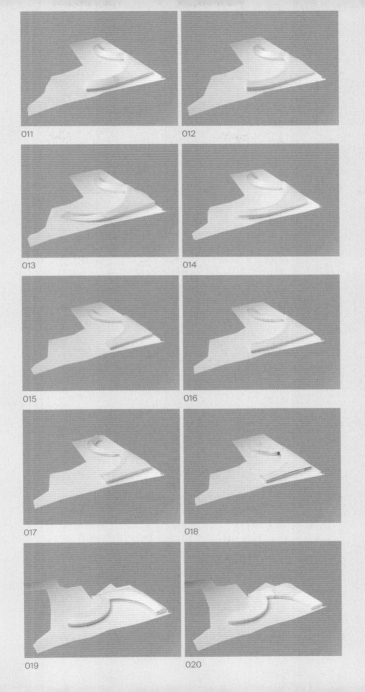

1	Entrance	1	玄関
2	Hall	2	ホール
3	0-year old children's room	3	0歳児保育室
4	1-year old children's room	4	1歳児保育室
5	Room for children's from 3 to 5 years old	5	3,4,5歳児保育室
6	Parenting support office	6	子育て支援室
7	Teachers' room	7	職員室
8	Principal's room	8	園長室
9	Reception room	9	応接室
10	Kitchen	10	調理室
11	Storage	11	倉庫
12	Playground	12	園庭
13	Parking lot	13	駐車場
14	Shrine	14	神社

● Plan. In order to provide separate activity spaces according to the development level of children's physical abilities, the playground is divided in two sections that are respectively connected to nursery rooms of different age groups, namely a younger children's group (0,1 and 2 years old) and older children's group (3,4 and 5 years old).

● 平面図。身体能力の発達に応じて異なる保育空間を与えるため庭を大きくふたつに分け、0,1,2歳児の保育室と3,4,5歳児のための保育室がそれぞれ向かい合う

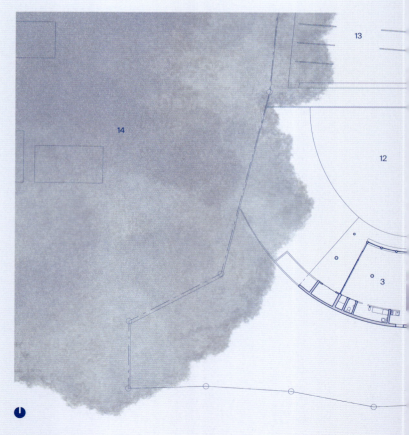

Plan | 平面図 | 1:500

Site plan | 配置図 | 1:10000

白地は市街化区域、
白地以外は市街化調整区域を示す。
西に神社の鎮守の森、
北東に花立山を眺めることができる。

The white area indicates an
urbanization promotion area.
The other area indicates an
urbanization control area.
One can see the sacred grove
towards west and Hanatate
Mountain towards northeast.

369

すばる保育園

71

● Playground with the adjoining sacred grove of a local shrine in the background.

● 隣接する神社の鎮守の森が借景となる園庭

すばる保育園

● Round columns with the diameter of 450mm support the roof slab. Benches are placed inside and outside along the windows.

● 450φの丸い柱がスラブを支える。
窓際には内外にベンチが置かれる

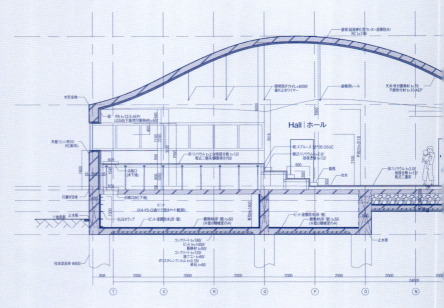

Section｜断面図｜1:150

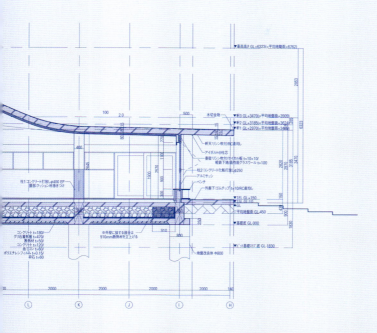

● Section of the hall. The 2-meter overhanging eave made of a 180mm-thick concrete slab is extended into the curved surface and form a roof above the hall.

● ホール断面図。t=180のコンクリートスラブが2m持ち出された軒先(右)からそのまま膨らんでホールの屋根となる

● A panoramic view of the landscape, framed by the horizontal window.
● 切り取られた開口から ランドスケープのパノラマが広がる

すばる保育園

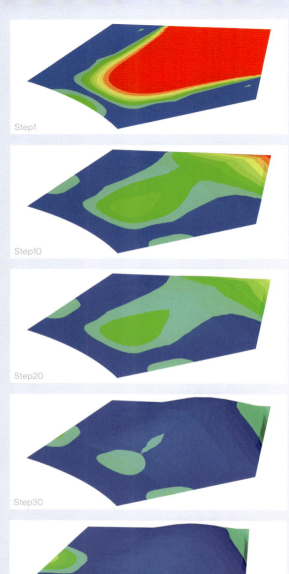

Dome structural analysis drawing｜ドーム構造解析図

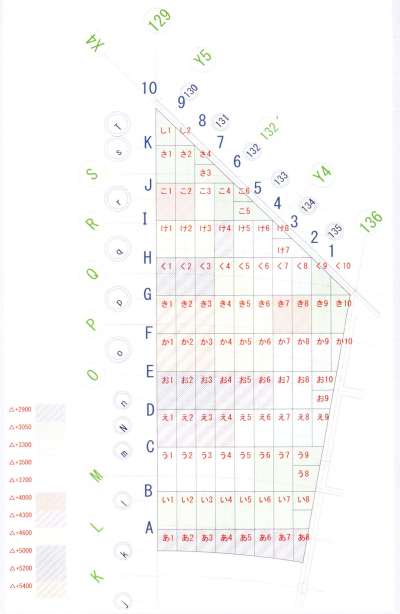

Formwork layout | パネル割

すばる保育園

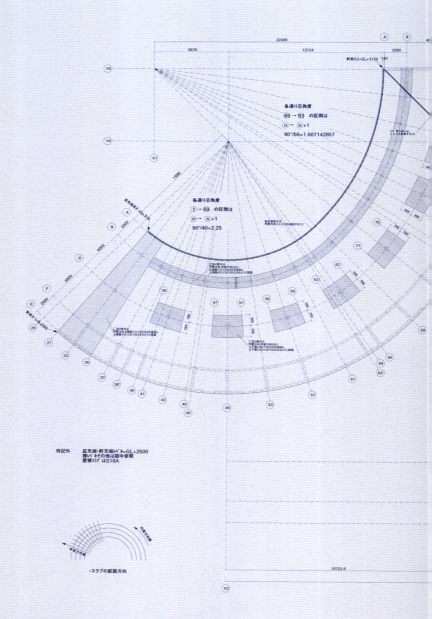

Roof reinforcement bar detail drawing｜屋根配筋詳細図

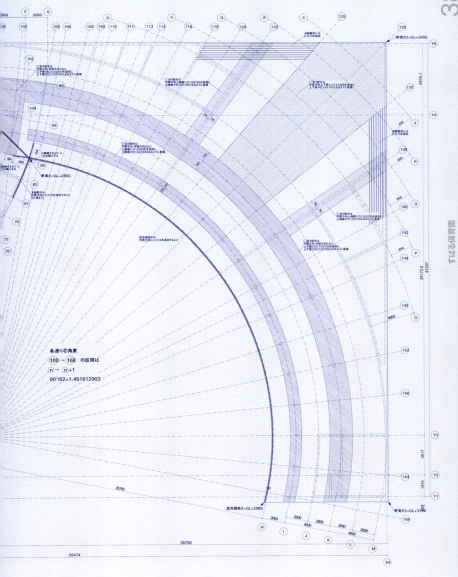

● Roof reinforcement bar detail drawing. The density steel reinforcement bars changes while the slab thickness stays the same.

● 屋根配筋詳細図。スラブ厚さは変わらないままに鉄筋の密度のみが変化する

● Undulation of the roof and the mountain correspond with each other.

● ホール屋根の膨らみと山の膨らみが一致した

Deep Learning Chair

アラビア語 Arabic			ベンガル語 Bengali			中国語 Chinese			英語 English			Hindi
a	b	c	a	b	c	a	b	c	a	b	c	a

スペイン語 Spanish			ロシア語 Russian			ポルトガル語 Portuguese			日本語 Japanese		
a	b	c	a	b	c	a	b	c	a	b	c

Deep Learning Chair

7.2 | Deep Learning Chair
is an evolutionary form of "G Chair" and an experimentation with substituting some part of the design process of a chair with machine-learning.

—

We aimed to further develop the "G Chair" experimentation using the following method. For a start, we made 3D models based on the nine most spoken languages (three types of chairs per language) totaling 27 pieces, changed their proportions parametrically and made a set of image data. The next step was to recreate these models through the process of deep learning using a machine language. Technically, image data were converted to voxel data and then recreated into optimum voxel data. Contrary to "Global G Chair" implemented by humans, this experiment was implemented through machine-learning.

—

I expected that this experiment would help us see our past design processes from an objective viewpoint. From what I observed, humans probably do better in the process of analyzing and extracting typologies. On the other hand, it seems that machines can bring more precise results in the process of recreating typical forms through calculations based on vast amounts of data.

—

When humans do the job, the results may be influenced by the level of empathy one has toward a person who brought the results. Sometimes empathy helped the process, but also hindered it otherwise. Although "Global G Chair" brought unique results, some people may find it ironic depending on how we present it.

—

The results generated through the machine-driven process appear more convincing. Machine-generated design based

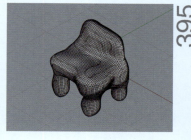

7.2 | Deep Learning Chair は、「G Chair」を進化させ椅子の設計作業の一部を機械学習に置き換える試みである。

「G Chair」の試みを以下の手順で発展させたいと考えた。まず上位9か国語で各3タイプ、合計27タイプを3Dモデル化し、プロポーションをパラメトリックに変化させて画像データのセットをつくる。それを機械言語で深層学習させて再現する。具体的には画像データからボクセルデータに置き換え、あり得べきボクセルデータを再現する。「Global G Chair」の人間版に対し、機械学習版である。

これによって、これまで自分がやってきたデザイン作業を鏡に映すことを期待した。分析して類型を取り出す作業は今のところ人間のほうが得意なようだ。でもそこから先の、大量のデータをもとに計算によって典型的なかたちを再現する作業は、機械に任せることでより確かな結果を引き出すことができそうだ。

人間がやると、結果の良しあしというよりは、その結果を導いた人間に対する共感の有無が問題になる。共感が可能にしていたこともあるが、阻んでいたこともある。「Global G Chair」も、ユニークな結果を得られたが、言い方によっては皮肉に受け取られてしまう。

でも機械が介在すると、もしかしたらあり得るかもしれないと思えるある種の説得力がある。データと計算が生み出すデザインは共感以外のコミュニケーションを可能にさせるのかもしれない。あるいは「すばる保育園」の屋根が周辺の山々に呼応しているように見えて私たちが笑いを禁じ得なかったように、機械言語によるデザインは新しいタイプのユーモアを生み出すのかもしれない。

396

7.2 Deep Learning Chair

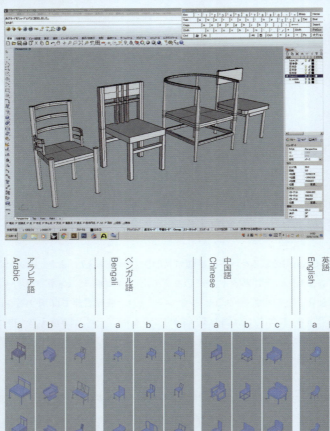

アラビア語 Arabic			ベンガル語 Bengali			中国語 Chinese			英語 English			Hindi
a	b	c	a	b	c	a	b	c	a	b	c	a

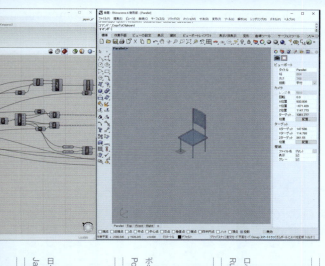

- Data sets were generated based on modeling data of "G Chair."
- 「G Chair」のモデリングデータをもとに生成された椅子のデータセット

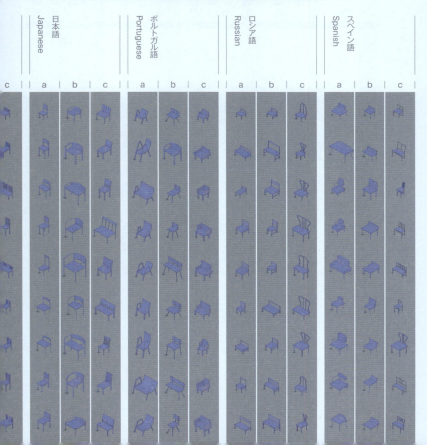

日本語 / Japanese
ポルトガル語 / Portuguese
ロシア語 / Russian
スペイン語 / Spanish

Deep Learning Chair

7.2

on data and calculation may successfully facilitate communication based on something other than empathy. I also expect that machine-generated design may conceive a new kind of humor — perhaps the same kind of humor that made us laugh when we spotted unexpected correspondence between the shape of the roof and the undulating mountain.

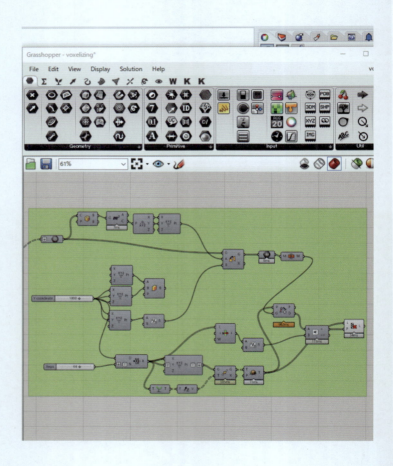

- The modeling data of "G chair" was converted into a set of voxels.
- 「G Chair」のモデリングデータをボクセルの集合に置換する

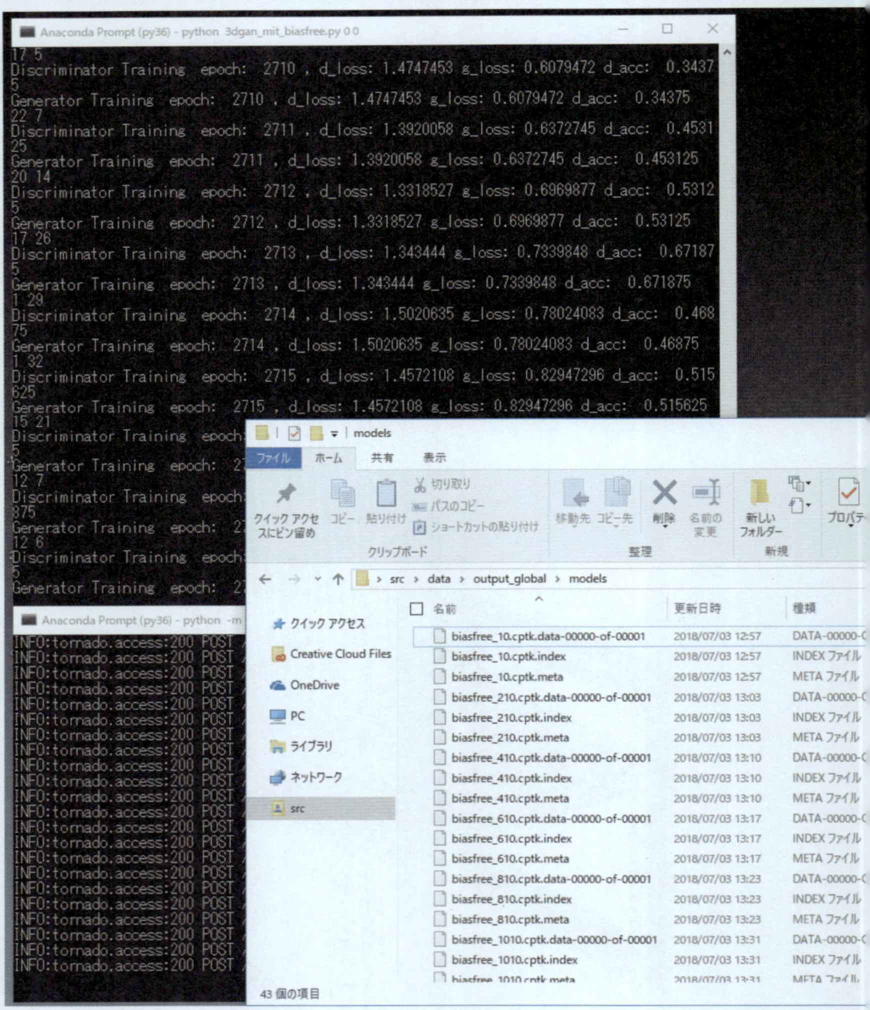
Anaconda Prompt (py36) - python 3dgan_mit_biasfree.py 0 0
17 5
Discriminator Training epoch: 2710 , d_loss: 1.4747453 g_loss: 0.6079472 d_acc: 0.3437
5
Generator Training epoch: 2710 , d_loss: 1.4747453 g_loss: 0.6079472 d_acc: 0.34375
22 7
Discriminator Training epoch: 2711 , d_loss: 1.3920058 g_loss: 0.6372745 d_acc: 0.4531
25
Generator Training epoch: 2711 , d_loss: 1.3920058 g_loss: 0.6372745 d_acc: 0.453125
20 14
Discriminator Training epoch: 2712 , d_loss: 1.3318527 g_loss: 0.6969877 d_acc: 0.5312
5
Generator Training epoch: 2712 , d_loss: 1.3318527 g_loss: 0.6969877 d_acc: 0.53125
17 26
Discriminator Training epoch: 2713 , d_loss: 1.343444 g_loss: 0.7339848 d_acc: 0.67187
5
Generator Training epoch: 2713 , d_loss: 1.343444 g_loss: 0.7339848 d_acc: 0.671875
1 29
Discriminator Training epoch: 2714 , d_loss: 1.5020635 g_loss: 0.78024083 d_acc: 0.468
75
Generator Training epoch: 2714 , d_loss: 1.5020635 g_loss: 0.78024083 d_acc: 0.46875
1 32
Discriminator Training epoch: 2715 , d_loss: 1.4572108 g_loss: 0.82947296 d_acc: 0.515
625
Generator Training epoch: 2715 , d_loss: 1.4572108 g_loss: 0.82947296 d_acc: 0.515625
Anaconda Prompt (py36) - python -m
INFO:tornado.access:200 POST
models
ファイル
ホーム
共有
表示
クイック アクセスにピン留め
コピー
貼り付け
切り取り
パスのコピー
ショートカットの貼り付け
クリップボード
移動先
コピー先
削除
名前の変更
整理
新しいフォルダー
新規
プロパティ
src › data › output_global › models
クイック アクセス
Creative Cloud Files
OneDrive
PC
ライブラリ
ネットワーク
src
名前
更新日時
種類
biasfree_10.cptk.data-00000-of-00001 2018/07/03 12:57
biasfree_10.cptk.index 2018/07/03 12:57 INDEX ファイル
biasfree_10.cptk.meta 2018/07/03 12:57 META ファイル
biasfree_210.cptk.data-00000-of-00001 2018/07/03 13:03
biasfree_210.cptk.index 2018/07/03 13:03 INDEX ファイル
biasfree_210.cptk.meta 2018/07/03 13:03 META ファイル
biasfree_410.cptk.data-00000-of-00001 2018/07/03 13:10
biasfree_410.cptk.index 2018/07/03 13:10 INDEX ファイル
biasfree_410.cptk.meta 2018/07/03 13:10 META ファイル
biasfree_610.cptk.data-00000-of-00001 2018/07/03 13:17
biasfree_610.cptk.index 2018/07/03 13:17 INDEX ファイル
biasfree_610.cptk.meta 2018/07/03 13:17 META ファイル
biasfree_810.cptk.data-00000-of-00001 2018/07/03 13:23
biasfree_810.cptk.index 2018/07/03 13:23 INDEX ファイル
biasfree_810.cptk.meta 2018/07/03 13:23 META ファイル
biasfree_1010.cptk.data-00000-of-00001 2018/07/03 13:31
biasfree_1010.cptk.index 2018/07/03 13:31 INDEX ファイル
43 個の項目

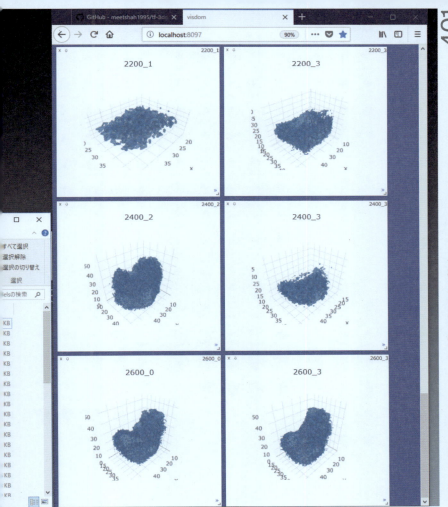

● Experiments in generation of chairs using deep learning. The number of times deep learning is repeated was gradually increased and results were compared (experimented in collaboration with Junichiro Horikawa).

● 深層学習による椅子の生成の試行。
学習の回数を徐々に増やして結果を比較する
(協力:堀川淳一郎)

Deep Learning Chair

Arabic ｜ アラビア語

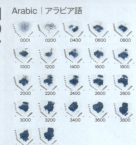

Bengali ｜ ベンガル語

Chinese ｜ 中国語

English ｜ 英語

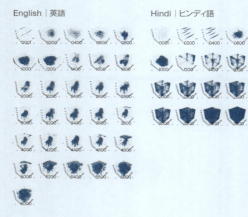

Hindi ｜ ヒンディ語

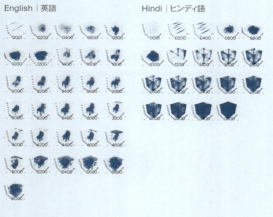

Japanese ｜ 日本語

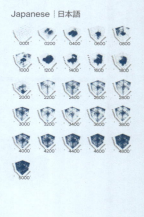

Portuguese ｜ ポルトガル語

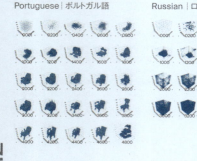

Russian ｜ ロシア語

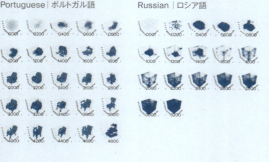

Spanish ｜ スペイン語

● Results of computational generation of chairs based on data sets in respective languages.

● 言語別のデータセットをもとにした深層学習による椅子の生成結果

● Data of a chair generated through deep learning based on the data sets in the nine most spoken languages.

● 上位9か国語別の椅子のデータセットをもとに深層学習を行い、生成された椅子のデータ

Deep Learning Chair

403

7.2

404

7.2 Deep Learning Chair

Arabic | アラビア語

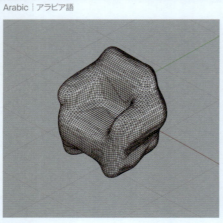

Bengali | ベンガル語

English | 英語

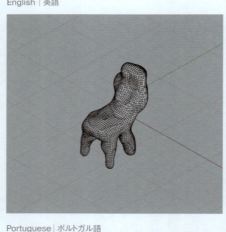

Hindi | ヒンディ語

Portuguese | ポルトガル語

Russian | ロシア語

Chinese | 中国語

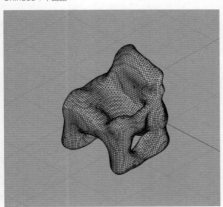

Japanese | 日本語

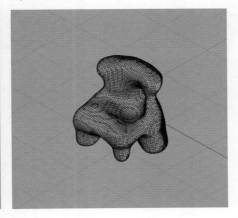

Spanish | スペイン語

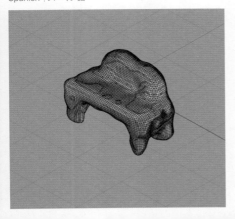

● Smooth-shaped chairs generated based on voxel data in the nine most spoken languages.

● 上位9か国語別の椅子の ボクセルデータをもとに生成された なめらかな椅子

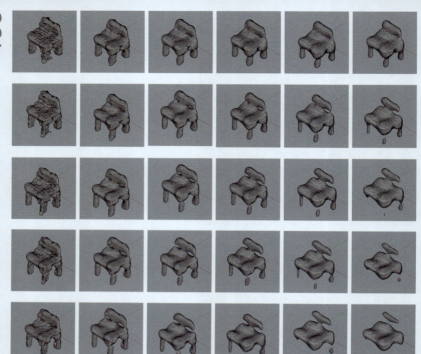

- Smooth-shaped chairs generated through deep learning based on data sets in the nine most spoken languages.

- 上位9か国語のすべての データセットをもとに 深層学習によって生成された なめらかな椅子

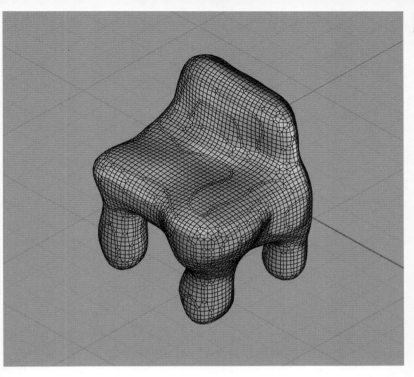

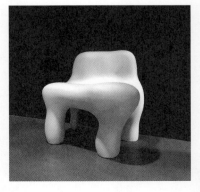

- Final Model
- 最終案

Deep Learning Chair

7.3 | Architecture as A Form of Knowledge

In this book, my exploration into architecture as a "form of knowledge" has evolved in the following ways:

1. Regarding application of knowledge in architecture, our approach has evolved from an "individual-based" session through informal dialogues to a "collective" session through formal procedures including workshops and votes in order to expand the scale of communication.

2. Regarding recognition of forms in architecture, our approach has evolved from a "semiotic" thinking based on patterns of forms embedded in peoples' conventions and memories to a new way of thinking based on the concept of architecture as a "continuous body" comprising geometric forms and configurations.

To summarize my exploration, the "form of knowledge" are categorized in four prototypes as follows:

- Prototype a: Individual "knowledge" and semiotic "form." Example: BUILDING K, House HOUSE
- Prototype b: Individual "knowledge" and continuous "form." Example: Shop U, APARTMENT N, Subaru Nursery School
- Prototype c: Collective "knowledge" and semiotic "form." Example: Facility for Ecology Education
- Prototype d: Collective "knowledge" and continuous "form." Example: OM TERRACE

My exploration on the "form of knowledge", which originated in individual and semiotic thinking of "Prototype a", will focus mainly on more complex issues based on collective and continuous thinking of "Prototype d" from now on.

Another experimental approach to expanding the scale of communication is to employ deeplearning processes to make continuous forms based on computational "knowledge (data)" automatically generated through the use of search en-

| 7.3 | 「ちのかたち」としての建築

本書において「ちのかたち」としての建築をめぐる探求は、以下のように発展してきた。

1. 「ち（知識）」に関する発展は、テーブルでの会話のような、インフォーマルな対話による「個人的な」セッションから、ワークショップや投票などルールを定めたフォーマルな対話による「集団的な」セッションへと、コミュニケーションのスケールを拡張することであった。

2. 「かたち（形態）」に関する発展は、人びとの慣習的な形態の記憶をパターン化した「記号的なもの」をベースにした認知から、幾何学や図形を用いた「連続的なもの」をベースにした認知へと展開することであった。

これらをまとめると私の探求における「ちのかたち」は、概ね以下の4つの類型に分けられた。

- 類型a：個人的な「ち」かつ記号的な「かたち」
  例：BUILDING K、家の家
- 類型b：個人的な「ち」かつ連続的な「かたち」
  例：SHOP U、APARTMENT N、すばる保育園
- 類型c：集団的な「ち」かつ記号的な「かたち」
  例：鶴ヶ島太陽光発電所環境教育施設
- 類型d：集団的な「ち」かつ連続的な「かたち」
  例：OM TERRACE

「ちのかたち」をめぐる探求は個人的かつ記号的な「類型a」からスタートしたが、今後はより複雑な、集団的かつ連続的な「類型d」こそが、取り組んでいくべき課題となるだろう。

さらに検索エンジンや3D作図ソフト、シミュレーションを用いて生成した計算的な「ち（データ）」をもとに、深層学習を用いて連続的な「かたち」を導いていき、デジタルな「ちのかたち」を生成することでコミュニケーションのスケールを拡大する試みが以下である。

gines, 3D CAD software, and simulationsin order to create a digital "form of knowledge", which is categorized as follows:

- • Prototype e: Computational "knowledge" and semiotic "forms." Example: G Chair
- • Prototype f: Computational "knowledge" and continuous "forms." Example: Deep Learning Chair

These prototypes will hopefully enable us to realize architecture as a "form of knowledge" based on direct and deep dialogues with individuals and committees or the public through workshops and voting without resorting to conventional decision-making systems. We may have a dialogue not only with people but also with fauna and flora or the surrounding environment itself. Architecture as the ultimate "form of knowledge" is the embodiment of "architecture for all people and things" composed of elements constituting all environments related to the architecture itself.

The engineering-based open approach employing intensive applications of machine language and calculations as well as articulate procedures contributes largely to the realization of the "form of knowledge." Strict adherence to "Engineering-ism" will promote the eradication of dominance by "verbal human communication" — often prolonged by behaviors such as intimidating others with loud voices or continuing meaningless arguments solely for the sake of protecting one's position — from the realization process of architecture. I would like to clarify my point below by comparing contexts of logic and architecture.

How can we explain how to design "a Form of knowledge"? As previously explained in this book, I experimentally introduced design patterns "Super Linear Design Process" based on the principle of "no jumping" "no branching out" and "no going back" into the design process following the procedures below:

1. Carry out "prototyping" that gives the form of a moment by using medium such as models based on information that was known or obvious requests
2. Carry out a "feedback" that removes misfits between

- 類型 e：計算的な「ち」かつ記号的な「かたち」
  例：G Chair
- 類型 f：計算的な「ち」かつ連続的な「かたち」
  例：Deep Learning Chair

—

これらを用いれば、個人への仮託や委員会、ワークショップや投票など、従来の意思決定システムとは異なるかたちで、意見の違いや意思決定など政治に関する差異も、コストやバランスなど経済に関する差異も、地域性やローカリティなど文化に関する差異も反映した、直接的かつ深層的な対話による「ちのかたち」としての建築をつくることができるかもしれない。対話の相手は、人だけではなく、ときに動植物であったり、環境そのものであるかもしれない。究極の「ちのかたち」としての建築は、その建築に関わるすべての環境を構成する要素による、「すべての人ともののための建築」を実現することである。

—

手続きを明快にする開かれた工学のあり方とその進化は、「ちのかたち」の形成に大きく貢献する。工学主義に徹することは、建築のプロセスから、大きな声で場を制圧するようなパフォーマンスや、立場を守るための議論のための議論、長い時間をかけてセッションするような「人間による、言葉によるコミュニケーション」の支配を打ち消すであろう。

—

「ちのかたち」はどのように生み出すと説明し得るか。私は本書でみてきたように設計のプロセスに「ジャンプしない」「枝分かれしない」「後戻りしない」をルールとしたパタン「超線形設計プロセス」を導入してきた。それらは以下のような手順で行われた。

—

1. 知り得た情報や明らかな要求をもとに模型などのメディウムを用いて、とりあえずの形状を与える「プロトタイピング」を行う
2. 与えられた形状と文脈の不整合の不一致を取り除いて「規則」を追加する「フィードバック」を行う
3. 1-2を繰り返し、得られた規則の束からそもそもの目的を推論し、得られた形の確からしさを上げていく

—

C.S. パースの論理学では、推論の形式を以下のように定義する。

—

- 演繹（deduction）：分析的推論──前提の内容に含まれている情報

the form and the context and add "rules"

3. Repeat steps 1 and 2, infer the purpose of the original from the bundle of rules obtained, and increase the certainty of the obtained form

Inference methods in Charles Sanders Peirce (1839-1914)'s logic are defined as follows:

- Deduction: Analytic Inference (elucidating the information contained in the contents of the premise)
- Induction: Ampliative Inference (generalization from experiences)
- Abduction: Ampliative Inference (devising hypotheses and theories)

The "Functionalism" in which forms and functions are tied based on the "standard" rules established by surveys, and the design schemes are created deductively, became established in the process of modernization society. On the other hand, some architects criticized the rigidity of the design schemes based on the above-mentioned method and strived to conceive works using different methods, many of which were explained as products of their "personal intuitions." The "abductive leap" in Pierce's "abduction" had functioned effectively to explain the creativity claimed by the architects.

However, in modern society where the premise of functionalism is at stake due to the advance of globalization and informatization, could it be really effective to insist on introducing "abductive leaps" as the basis of creativity in the design processes, based on their personal experiences?

The "Super Linear Design Process" which compares observable phenomena of the same class by models, although it is an ampliative inference, is closer to "induction" which generalizes based on experience than to "abduction" which forms a hypothesis for explaining observation, as a form of logic. I find new creativity that is different from rigidity of functionalism and also oligopoly of anti-functionalism in the extension of knowledge by "inductive leap." Since it is an ampliative inference unlike analytic inference "deduc-

を解明する

- 　　帰納（induction）：拡張的推論——経験から一般化を行う
- 　　アブダクション（abduction）：拡張的推論——仮説や理論を発案

—

調査によって定められた「標準」という規則に基づいて形態と機能が結ばれ、演繹的に設計案が作成される「機能主義」は、近代化の過程で社会に定着した。対して建築家は、そのように定められる設計案の硬直性を批判し、異なる方法で設計案を得ようとしてきたが、それらの多くは「個人の直感」による推論であると説明してきた。パースの「アブダクション」における「仮説的飛躍 abductive leap」は、建築家の主張する創造性を説明するには有効に機能してきた。

—

しかし、グローバル化や情報化が進み機能主義の前提が揺らぐ現代社会において、設計プロセスに建築家個人の経験に基づく「仮説的飛躍 abductive leap」の導入を創造性の根拠として主張することは本当に有効だろうか。

—

拡張的推論ではあるが、模型などによる同種の観察可能な事象群の比較を行う「超線形設計プロセス」は、論理の形式としては観察を説明するための仮説を形成する「アブダクション」よりは、観察に基づく経験の一般化を行う「帰納」に近いと考えられる。機能主義の硬直とも、反機能主義の寡占とも異なる新しい創造性を「帰納的飛躍 inductive leap」による知識の拡張に見出す。分析的推論である「演繹」とは異なり拡張的推論である以上設計の可能性は実践とともに拡張し、ステップごとに「アブダクション」のような大きな飛躍を伴わないため多様な主体によるコレクティブな設計により適しているからである。

—

ここで従来の機能主義、反機能主義に対して「工学主義」を仮定すると、推論の形式の違いから以下のように区別される。

—

- 　　機能主義の建築：「標準」という規則を用いる分析的推論（演繹）
- 　　反機能主義の建築：個人の直感に基づいた拡張的推論（アブダクション）
- 　　工学主義の建築：反復手続きによる比較に基づいた拡張的推論（帰納）

—

以上より、「ちのかたち」としての建築とは、機能主義における形態と機能の因果関係が揺らぐ現代社会で確かな拡張的推論の手法としての「超線形設計プロセス」を用いることで機能主義、反機能主義のいずれとも異なる「工学主義」の立場を取ることを指す、というのが本書のさしあたりの結論である。

tive", the possibility of design extends with practice and there is no big leap in each step like "abduction." It is a more suitable method for collective design.

"Engineering-ism" is hereby differentiated from Functionalism and Anti-functionalism based on the difference of respective forms of logic as follows:

- Functionalist architecture: Analytical Inference using the rule of "standards" (Deduction)
- Anti-functionalist architecture: Ampliative Inference based on personal intuition (Abduction)
- Engineering-ism architecture: Ampliative Inference based on iterative procedure comparison (Induction)

Based on findings in my ongoing exploration described above, I would like to conclude, for the time being, that by using the "Super Linear Design Process" as a reliable ampliative inference method in contemporary society where the causal relation of form and function in functionalism is unstable, it is possible to take a position of "engineering-ism" different from functionalism and anti-functionalism in this book.

In principle, "engineering" is regarded as an effective method of achieving our goal. However, we should keep in mind that we often take a wrong direction by uncritically employing engineering in today's society heavily dependent on engineering — as was revealed in the Fukushima Daiichi Nuclear Power Plant disaster. We architects, who strive to realize the "form of knowledge", are expected to positively embrace engineering and yet simultaneously maintain a critical attitude in its application. I am going to term such stance as "Critical Engineering-ism." Critical Engineering-ism is a major premise in the realization of architecture as a "form of knowledge."

It is needless to say that we have to apply the concept of the "form of knowledge" in many more cases and obtain as much feedback as possible in order to successfully develop one of reliable methodologies that will effectively help maintain diversity in our highly segmentalized and integrated post-modernization society.

ここで「工学」はその方法として原則肯定されている。ただし、福島第一原子力発電所の事故が明らかにしたように、工学に大きく依存した現代の社会において、工学を無批判に用いることはしばしば、私たちに大きく方向を誤らせることがある。工学を半ば肯定しつつ、半ば批判的に使用する態度がよりいっそう私たち「ちのかたち」をつくり出そうとするアーキテクトに求められるだろう。私はそのような態度を「批判的工学主義」と呼ぼうとしている。批判的工学主義は「ちのかたち」としての建築の、大きな前提である。

—   —

「ちのかたち」を高度に細分化、集積化が進んだ近代以後の社会で多様性を維持する確かな方法論とするためには、今後より多くの場面での応用とフィードバックを必要とすることは言うまでもない。

7.4 | Axis of Hope

7.4 | 希望の軸

● The Japan Archipelago is considered as an architecture. Now that "remodeling" of the Japan Archipelago has subsided, one can apply skills gained through the process to "remodeling" of the Asian archipelago. The answer to the "axis of Question" may be found on the extended axis. It was named "Axis of Hope."

● 日本列島をひとつの建築として考える。
日本列島の改造が一段落した今、
そこで得たスキルはアジアの列島改造に生かされる。
「問いの軸」(p.028)の答えはその延長線上にある。
「希望の軸」と名付けられた

8.0 Drawing a line - Architectural Thinking of Ryui Fujimura

—

Yoshikazu Nango

Associate Professor, School of Information and Communication, Meiji University
Sociology, Theory of Urbanism and Architecture
Born in 1979, Osaka, JAPAN

—

Biography

2017–	Associate Professor, School of Information and Communication, Meiji University
2012-2017	Assistant Professor, School of Information and Communication, Meiji University
2011–2012	Project Lecturer, Interfaculty Initiative in Information Studies, The University of Tokyo
2008-2011	Research Associate, Interfaculty Initiative in Information Studies, The University of Toky
2008	Withdrew from the Ph.D. program with the completion of course requirements, Graduate School of Interdisciplinary Information Studies, The University of Tokyo

8.0 線を引くこと──藤村龍至の建築的思考

南後由和

明治大学情報コミュニケーション学部 准教授／社会学、都市・建築論
1979年大阪府生まれ／東京大学大学院学際情報学府博士課程単位取得退学
主な著書に『ひとり空間の都市論』（ちくま新書、2018）、『商業空間は何の夢を見たか』（共著、平凡社、2016）、
『建築の際』（編、平凡社、2015）、『文化人とは何か?』（共編、東京書籍、2010）など。

Architects should grasp an atmosphere of the times and draw a line once again — a symbolic line transcending time and space while connecting the farthest possible points.

Drawing Using Models

An architect's competence is displayed in where and how he/she draws a line and what kind of line he/she draws. Ever since the establishment of the architectural profession in the Renaissance period, sketches and drawings have been considered a creative medium communicating signature characteristics of architects. The architects' hand drawings have been mythicized as the ultimate source of creativity because drawings are generally attributed to a sole individual (architect) and others were not allowed to be involved in the making process.

Fujimura, on the other hand, clearly defines the process of collective design open to all individuals and make full use of models as its effective tool. In his view, the act of making models is related to the act of drawing a line. "Super Linear Design Process" is the design process conceived and coined by Fujimura, which starts with placing a simple volume model. Models evolve and increase the level of complexity through a series of meetings and workshops while serving as a medium to record and accumulate communication logs between the parties involved.

Making reference to Christopher Alexander, Fujimura's models may be interpreted as a "diagram" (pattern) bridging design requirements and forms. Or they may be intended to serve as "Google Spatial Translate", following a project title coined by Fujimura himself. Fujimura strives to correlate architecture with different fields including politics, economics and welfare in an ingenious way and translates various issues in respective fields into visual expression in architecture.

Fujimura's models may be associated with MVRDV's presentation method. Winy Maas, one of the co-founders of the Dutch architectural practice, was Fujimura's mentor at the former Berlage Institute. MVRDV devised a presenta-

建築家は今いちど、時代の空気を読み、線を引くべきなのである。それもできるだけ遠くにあるもの同士を結び付け、時間や空間を超えるようなシンボリックな線を[1]。

模型によるドローイング

—

建築家の腕の見せどころは、どこに、いかに、どのような線を引くかにある。ルネサンス期に建築家の職能が確立して以来、建築家の署名性は、スケッチや図面などのドローイングに宿るとされてきた。一般的にドローイングとは、建築家という個人に閉じられ、他者がその創作プロセスに関与することができないものとしてある。ゆえに、建築家の手によって紡ぎ出されるドローイングは、創造の源として神秘化されてきた。

—

それに対し、藤村は、手続きが明確化され、他者に開かれた集団的設計のツールとして模型を駆使する。ただし、藤村にとって、模型は線を引くことと無縁ではない。「超線形設計プロセス」と名付けられた設計プロセスは、単純な形式とボリュームの模型を置くところから始まる。ミーティングやワークショップの回数を重ねるごとに、個々の要求やコンテクストが形に反映され、模型は複雑性を増しながら進化していく。模型は、他者とのコミュニケーションを履歴として蓄積、保存したメディウムである。

—

クリストファー・アレグザンダーに倣うなら、藤村にとっての模型は要求と形との間を橋渡しする「ダイアグラム（パタン）」を兼ね備えているといえるだろうし[2]、藤村自身のプロジェクト名に倣うなら、それは要求が入力されると空間的に翻訳される'Google Spatial Translate'を志向しているといえるかもしれない。藤村は、建築と政治、経済、福祉などの領域を巧みに結び付け、それらの諸問題を、建築に置き換えて可視化しようとする。

—

ここで想起されるのは、オランダの建築家MVRDVのプレゼンテーションである——藤村はベルラーヘ・インスティテュート留学時代に、ヴィニー・マースに師事している。MVRDVは、データをダイアグラムによって視覚化し、1枚のシートにワンヴィジュアル＋ワンセンテンスで、リサーチから提案に至るまでのプロセスをリニアに提示する手法を編み出した。藤村はこの手法を、模型というメディウムに置き換えて展開している。

—

tion method of showing the entire process linearly from research to a proposal using a set of presentation sheets containing one visual image and one sentence per sheet. Fujimura is developing this method further by replacing the medium (graphic images) with models.

Interestingly, one can observe a line traversing across all the models when they are laid out in chronological order. The line is a trajectory of the collective decision-making process. It was drawn collectively by the hands of all parties involved, including specialists such as structural and building service engineers and contractors, the client and community residents, without involving an egoistic decision-making of a sole individual (architect). In other words, Fujimura is drawing a line using models. The line can be shared collectively and help provide all those involved with a greater sense of ownership of the architectural design. Fujimura may be viewed as developing further the idea of "Public Drawing" by Atelier Bow-Wow using models.

One should note, however, that Fujimura not only focuses on people in front of him who were present at the decision-making moment, but also strives to develop a method of collective design by integrating diverse collective knowledge of people including "invisible clients" connected through social media.

Bernard Tschumi once stated, "Architecture is not so much a knowledge of form, but a form of knowledge." For Fujimura, "architecture is a form of collective knowledge." He is actively applying his architectural thinking of giving form to collective knowledge in various occasions including exhibition curation, architectural education in universities and administrative reforms transcending boundaries between different organizations.

Line Cutting Through the Times

Fujimura is also determined to draw a line cutting through the times. His determination is apparent in his book, After 1995 and also exemplified by his standpoint in *"Critical Engineering-ism". Critical Engineering-ism* is one of the fruits

興味深いのは、一連の模型を時系列に並べると、それらの模型を横断して線が浮かび上がることだ。その線は、集団による意思決定の軌跡である。それは個人である建築家の独断ではなく、構造、設備、施工者などの専門家、施主や住民などとともに集団で引いた線である。藤村は、いわば模型を使って、線を引いているのだ。その線は、集団で共有可能なものであり、人びとによる建築のオーナーシップの獲得につながっている。アトリエ・ワンの「パブリック・ドローイング」を、藤村の場合は、模型を使って実践しているともいえる。

ただし、藤村の視野にあるのは、意思決定の場に居合わせる目の前の人びとだけではない。ソーシャル・メディアで接続された「見えないクライアント」を含めた、多種多様な集合知を統合し、かたちを与えていく集団設計の手法を追求している。

かつてベルナール・チュミは、「建築とは、かたちの知というよりも、知のかたちである」と述べたが[3]、藤村にとって、建築とは「集合知のかたち」としてある。現に藤村は「集合知」にかたちを与える建築的思考を、展覧会のキュレーション、大学での設計教育、さらには自治体における組織の垣根を超えた行政改革などへと積極的に応用している。

時代の切断線

藤村は、時代にも切断線を引こうとする。その姿勢は、藤村の編著本『1995年以後』という書名のほか、「批判的工学主義」という立場にも表れている——批判的工学主義は、藤村と社会学者である私の対話の産物のひとつでもある。

ル・コルビュジエは、1920年代の「工業化」を背景に、機能主義を受け入れつつ、それを戦略的に再構成する「批判的機能主義」とも呼べる建築運動を展開した。それに対し、藤村は1990年代後半以降の「情報化」を背景に、法規、市場原理、ビッグデータなどの諸条件によって半自動的に建築が出来上がってしまうような状況下において、それらの諸条件を戦略的に再構成する「批判的工学主義」の立場を掲げる。

criticalという英語は、"危機"の派生語であり、語源であるラテン語 criticus やギリシア語 kritikos は、"判断する・決定する"という意味をもっている[4]。批判的であることは、危機における判断や決定という態度を要請する。

of collaboration between Fujimura and myself who is a sociologist.

—

Le Corbusier led an architectural movement during the period of "industrialization" in the 1920's, in which he accepted functionalism and strategically reorganized it into a concept that could be termed as "Critical Functionalism." In contrast, Fujimura manifested his vision of "Critical Engineering-ism" in architecture during the period of "informatization" in the latter half of the 1990's: faced with a situation where architecture was shaped almost automatically according to various restrictive conditions including laws and regulations, market forces and big data analysis, he suggested that these conditions should be dismantled and reorganized critically and strategically in order to overcome issues arising from the current trend of "Engineering-ism."

—

The word "critical" is a derivative from "crisis", which is derived from the Latin word "*criticus*" and also the Greek word "*kritikos*" meaning "to judge" or "to decide." Therefore, being critical requires a person to commit him/herself to "judge and decide" at a moment of crisis.

—

If this is the case, what does Fujimura perceive as a crisis and what kind of judgement and decision does he intend to make? He is keenly aware of the question of how architecture and architects should survive in a transitional period influenced by advancement of informatization and globalization. In response, Fujimura made a judgement and decided to draw lines dividing eras through 1995, the year marked by the occurrence of the Great Hanshin Awaji Earthquake and the Tokyo subway sarin gas attack, as well as the release of Windows 95 and 2020, the year of Tokyo Olympics. He used these lines to express transformations in built forms and design methods responding to social changes in the respective eras. Fujimura's theories of "Critical Engineering-ism" and "Super Linear Design Process" are based on these types of judgements and decisions.

—

Gifted with the ability to grasp and understand an "atmosphere of the times", Fujimura is a rare architect with rich "Sociological Imagination." According to the American

では藤村は、何を危機として認識し、どのような判断や決定を下そうとしているのか。それは情報化やグローバル化の進展という時代の転換期に、いかにして建築および建築家が生き延びるのかという問題意識である。そして、阪神・淡路大震災や地下鉄サリン事件が起き、Windows95が発売された1995年、東京オリンピックが開かれる2020年に、時代の切断線を引き、それ以後の変化に対応した建築の型および建築家の手法を提示するという判断や決定である。批判的工学主義や超線形設計プロセス論も、このような判断や決定に裏打ちされている。

「時代の空気」を読むことに長けた藤村は、「社会学的想像力」を兼ね備えた稀有な建築家である。アメリカの社会学者ライト・ミルズによれば、「社会学的想像力」とは、個人の生を、歴史的変動や制度矛盾といった社会構造と結び付けて理解する力を指す[5]。実際、藤村の活動を見れば、埼玉県郊外のニュータウンで生まれ育ち、東京工業大学の社会工学科で住民参加型のまちづくりを学び、大学院では建築学専攻の塚本由晴研究室で建築の設計言語と形式を修得した自らの個人史と社会の動向を巧みに結び付け、設計活動へと昇華させていることがわかるだろう。

建築家の系譜という線

最後に、藤村を「建築家の系譜」に位置付けるべく、藤村と日本人建築家の足跡を線で結んでおこう。まず、藤村の建築に見られる構成論や抽象化への関心は、出身大学でもある東京工業大学の篠原一男、坂本一成や塚本由晴らの系譜に連なるものである。

ただし、藤村の特徴は、篠原スクールに、東京大学の丹下スクール──磯崎新、黒川紀章など──の文脈を交差させたところにあるように思われる。丹下健三は、「広島平和記念公園」において、平和記念資料館−慰霊碑−原爆ドームに軸線を引いた一方で、空間経済学的発想に基づき、日本という国土のあるべき姿を描こうとした。

丹下の時代は「高度成長期」であったが、藤村にとってのそれは「成熟・縮小期」である。丹下は、人口増加を背景に「足し算」として、東海道メガロポリスなどの大都市への投資という「集中モデル」を志向したのに対し、藤村は、人口

sociologist C. Wright Mills, the "Sociological Imagination" is an ability to understand historical change and social structures in relation to personal experiences. In fact, Fujimura's various activities prove that he ingeniously relates his own personal history — he was born and grew up in a suburban new town in Saitama Prefecture; studied citizen participatory urban planning at Department of Social Engineering, Tokyo Institute of Technology and studied at Yoshiharu Tsukamoto Laboratory at Graduate School of Architecture of the same university and acquired knowledge of the language and method of architectural design — with social trends to further develop and strengthen his architectural design.

Line Tracing the Genealogy of Japanese Architects

The final section aims to draw a line connecting Fujimura to the genealogy of Japanese architects. First of all, his interests in architectural composition theories and abstraction seen in his built work follows the genealogy of architects who graduated from Tokyo Institute of Technology, including Kazuo Shinohara, Kazunari Sakamoto and Yoshiharu Tsukamoto among others.

In my view, however, Fujimura's distinctive characteristics may be described as a cross between the Shinohara School and the Tange School represented by architects including Arata Isozaki and Kisho Kurokawa among others. Kenzo Tange drew a symbolic axis line connecting the Hiroshima Peace Memorial Museum, Memorial Cenotaph and A-Bomb Dome at the Hiroshima Peace Memorial Park, while presenting a grand vision for Japan's national land planning based on spatial economic concepts.

While Tange was active during the high economic growth period, Fujimura works in the maturing and aging society. As opposed to Tange's idea of the "concentration model" using the method of "addition" in the context of population growth where investments concentrated around megacities in Tokaido Megalopolis, Fujimura pushes forward the idea of the "dispersion model" of integrating and reorganizing public facilities transcending municipal boundaries using the method of "subtraction", in the context of depopulation

減少や施設老朽化などを背景に「引き算」として、市町村という行政単位を横断した公共施設の統合・再配置という「離散モデル」を志向し、「ポジティブな縮退」の道筋を探っている。そして、「希望の軸」に見られるような、国民国家の枠を超えたスケールで線を引くことによって、日本という国土が抱える複数の問題をアジアとの関係のなかで解こうとする。

—

また、「集合知のかたち」としての建築をめぐる一連のプロジェクトは、磯崎新の「孵化過程」や「海市」を、現代の情報社会の文脈においてバージョン・アップしたものであるし、時代に切断線を引き、歴史を物語る身振りも、磯崎のそれを継承したものであるといえる。

—

そのほか、雑誌とブログに分断された建築の議論の場を再設計することを企図したフリーペーパー『ROUNDABOUT JOURNAL』の刊行、Twitterなどのソーシャル・メディアを駆使して「動員」を促す姿は、一般の雑誌やテレビに頻繁に登場し、マスメディアを通じて建築の言説を流布させ、人びとの建築への関心を惹きつけることを得意とした黒川紀章を彷彿させる。

—

もちろん、時代の切断線にせよ、メディアを通したフレームの設定にせよ、線を引くということ、すなわち、何の問題を選択し、どのように切り取るかという行為は、政治と分かち難く結び付いている。藤村は、線をめぐる政治を引き受けた上で、線を引く建築的思考を多方面に展開しながら、これまでの建築家の歩みを前進させ、これからの時代の建築と建築家のかたちを描いている。

1｜藤村龍至, 2014,
『批判的工学主義の建築──
ソーシャル・アーキテクチャをめざして』
NTT出版, pp288-289.
Fujimura, Ryuji, 2014, *Critical Engineering-ism: Towards Social Architecture*, Tokyo: NTT Publishing.
2｜Alexander, Christopher, 1964, *Notes on the Synthesis of Form*, Cambridge, MA: Harvard University Press.

(＝2013, 稲葉武司・押野見邦英訳,『形の合成に関するノート／都市はツリーではない』鹿島出版会, p76)
3｜Tschumi, Bernard, 2014, "Architectural Manifestos", Craig Buckley ed., *After the Manifesto: Writing, Architecture, and Media in a New Century*, New York: GSAPP Books; Pamplona: T6) Ediciones, p181.
4｜Soanes, Catherine and

Angus Stevenson eds., 2003, *Oxford Dictionary of English*, Oxford; New York: Oxford University Press, pp410-411.
5｜Mills, C. W., 1959, *The Sociological Imagination*, New York: Oxford University Press.
(＝2017, 伊奈正人・中村好孝訳,『社会学的想像力』ちくま学芸文庫)

and building deterioration where he seeks possibilities for "positive degeneration." Moreover, he strives to solve Japan's various issues in relation to current situations in other Asian countries by drawing a line on a transnational scale as exemplified by his "Axis of Hope."

—

The series of his architectural projects implemented under the theme of "form of collective knowledge" may be understood as an upgraded version of Arata Isozaki's "Incubation Process" and "Mirage City" in the context of the contemporary information society. Fujimura's act of drawing a line cutting through the eras to narrate a history can be said to be a continuation of Isozaki's action.

—

Furthermore, Fujimura's willingness to influence and engage others through strategic uses of various media, such as publication of the free newspaper *ROUNDBOUNT JOURNAL* and his active involvement in social media including Twitter, may be associated with Kisho Kurokawa's skillful mass media manipulation through frequent appearances in magazines and television shows to spread his architectural theories and raise people's interest in architecture.

—

The act of drawing a line — whether dividing time or setting a view frame through media activity — is an act of deciding which issues should be selected and how they should be viewed, which is inseparably connected with politics. Fujimura actively takes political responsibility in drawing a line, pushes the boundaries of architectural profession and draws forms envisioning architecture and architects' roles in the coming era, while expanding his architectural thinking of "drawing a line" in multiple directions.

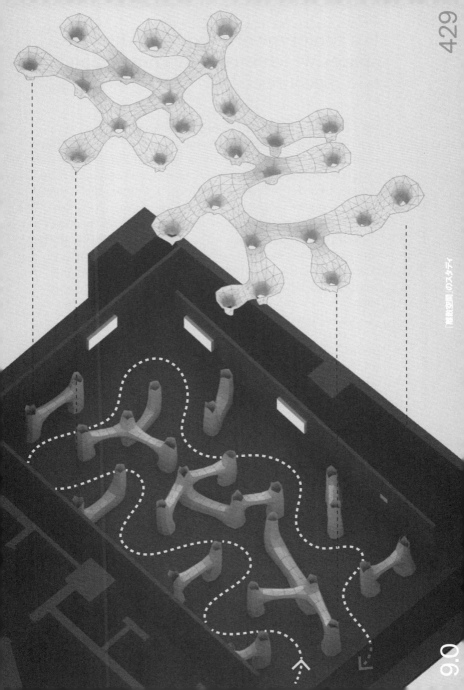

9.0 Study of "Discrete Space"
is a prototype of a model of discrete spaces which is equally connectable and disconnectable.

—

As a continuation of our approach to architecture, I am exploring new ways to study spaces where "what we think with our brains", "what we think with our hands" and "what we think based on calculations" are combined more equally in order to look at the "form of knowledge" from a new perspective. By actually making 1:1 mockups, we found that approximately six columns would be needed to support the 2.7 x 2.7m square space. We discussed with the cafe owner the possibility of using it as a coffee shop and changed column joints to build a space where small and complex sub-spaces connect, disconnect, and relate with each other in complex ways. This space was named the "Discrete Space C."

—

In order to make a more lightweight structure, we gave up the method of assembling a waffle structure made of corrugated cardboard and instead constructed a hollow structure using corrugated cardboard. The exhibition space of "The Form of Knowledge", constructed using the hollow structure, was named "Discrete Space G." This exhibition space showing seven video monitors and models were designed and built as a network of large structures based on "Discrete Space C." Here we intend to make a spatial model proposing a new public space in the future.

—

In the same way, we conceived an idea of "Discrete Space Furniture": these furniture pieces can be used in several ways at once, connect, disconnect, and relate with each other in complex ways. Based on this concept, we designed and built two types of furniture. A hanger rack called "Discrete Space Furniture H" for selling used clothes changes the height and width when used from different directions and offers three different ways of using it. A stand for selling coffee and sweets called "Discrete Space Furniture T" can be unfolded and used in several ways. The whole structure

9.0 │ 「離散空間」のスタディ
は、接続可能性と切断可能性が等価な
離散的な空間モデルのプロトタイプである

これまでの建築の延長で、新しい「ちのかたち」のあり方を模索するため、頭で考えたことと手で考えたことと計算で考えたことがもう少し等価に混ざったような、新しい空間のスタディの仕方を模索している。ここではまず3次元でスタディしたモデルをもとにダンボールをカットし、組み立てる2.7m立方のプロトタイプを設計した。実際に1/1のモックアップを制作してみると、全体が自立できるようにするためには2.7m四方の空間に柱が6本程度必要であることがわかった。コーヒーショップとして使えるようにカフェオーナーらと意見交換を行い、柱の連結方法を変化させて完成させた空間は、小さいが複数の空間が接続したり、切断したり、複雑なつながり方をしていた。この空間を「離散空間 C」と名付けた。

もっと軽量な構造体をつくるため、ダンボールでワッフル状に組み立てるのを止め、厚紙を利用した中空の構造体を作成し、「ちのかたち」の会場を構成したものを「離散空間 G」と名付けた。ここでは7台のモニターや模型類を展示する空間を構成するため、「離散空間 C」をもとにさらに大きな構造体をネットワークして、複雑なつながり方をした空間を設計し、制作した。パーソナルな空間とパブリックな空間の感覚が等価であるような、今後の公共空間のあり方を示唆する空間のモデルをつくろうとしている。

同様に、複数の使い方が同時に現れ、それらが接続したり、切断したり、複雑なつながり方をするような家具のあり方を「離散空間家具」と名付け、ふたつの家具を設計、制作した。古着などを販売するためのハンガーラック「離散空間家具H」は、使う向きを変えると高さや幅が変化し、3種類の使い方ができる。コーヒーやお菓子などを売るスタンド「離散空間家具T」は、広げて使うと複数の使い方が可能であるが、全体は冷蔵庫程度の大きさ(600×600×1,800)にコンパクトに収納し移動可能である。これらの家具は「ちのかたち」展終了後、東京郊外の「鳩山ニュータウン」と「椿峰ニュータウン」の公共空間で使われる。

can be collapsed into a refrigerator-size volume (600 x 600 x 1,800mm) and moved. After the exhibition ends, these furniture pieces will be used in public spaces at Hatoyama New Town and Tsubakimine New Town in the Suburbs of Tokyo.

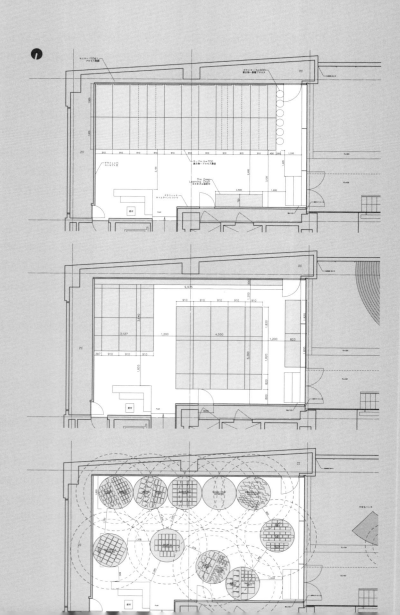

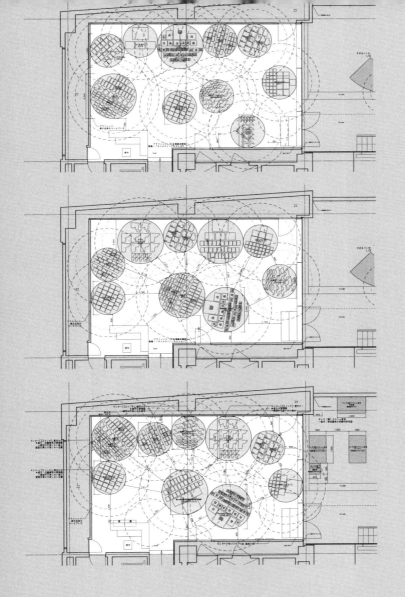

● Study of exhibition design for "Gallery 1"(3F) at TOTO GALLERY·MA. After making a proposal of laying out models in time sequence and another proposal of laying out models according to categories, we made a final proposal of using small and large tables to create a rhythm.

● TOTOギャラリー・間「ギャラリー1」(3階)の会場構成のスタディ。模型を時系列に並べる案、カテゴリー別に並べる案などを経て、大小のテーブルでリズムを生み出す案へと至る

Study of "Discrete Space"

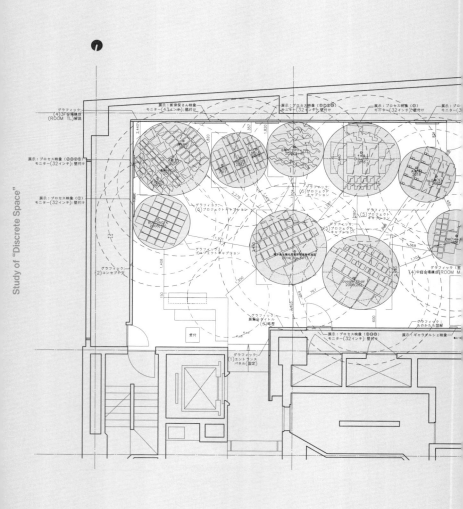

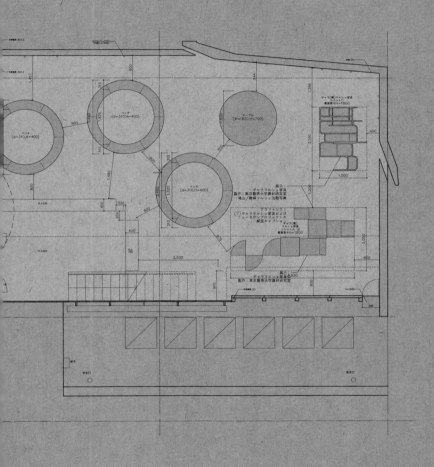

● Exhibition design of "Gallery 1" and the courtyard. Tables with the same sizes as the ones used inside are placed outside to create a sense of continuity. The courtyard is considered as a public square where marchés and talk events take place.

●「ギャラリー1」と中庭の会場構成。
屋外にも同じ大きさのテーブルを
並べて連続させる。
中庭は広場に見立てて
マルシェやトークイベントを開催する

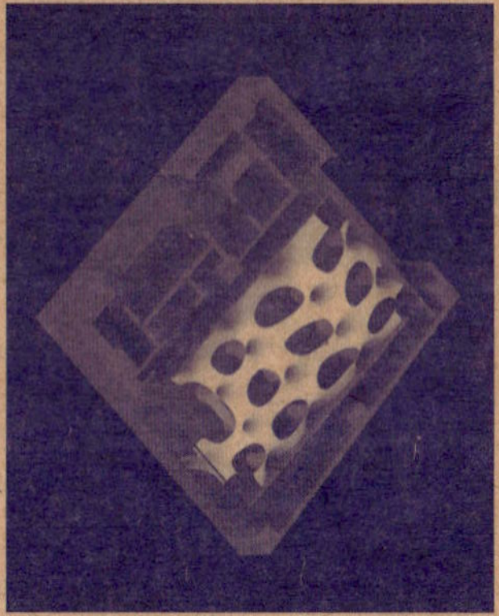

436

Study of "Discrete Space"

9.0

● Study of exhibition design for "Gallery 2" (4F) at TOTO GALLERY·MA. Based on the idea of "Discrete Space C", the entire space is open and loosely divided into seven separate subspaces displaying video monitors.

● TOTOギャラリー・間「ギャラリー2」(4階)の会場構成のスタディ。全体を連続させながら、7つの映像モニターのための空間に柔らかく分節する「離散空間C」を導入する

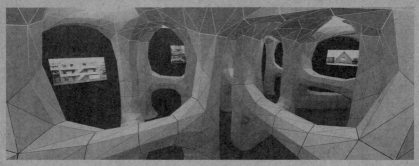

Design and Fabrication:
Fujimura Laboratory,
Tokyo University of the Arts

Riku Yamakawa
[Research associates]
Makoto Ohira
Haruka Inari
Mahiro Goto
Takahito Konishi
Fuka Nakahara
Ran Mo
Shuwei Cui
Chenkai Zhang
Hua Chen

設計・制作：
東京藝術大学藤村研究室

山川陸 [教育研究助手]
大平麻琴
稲荷悠
後藤眞皓
小西隆仁
中原風香
莫然
崔書維
張晨凱
陳華

「離散空間」のスタディ

ダンボール＋レーザーカット
Corrugated cardboard +
laser cutting

● Study of "Discrete Space C", a prototype for "Discrete Space G."

●「離散空間G」のプロトタイプとなった「離散空間C」のスタディ

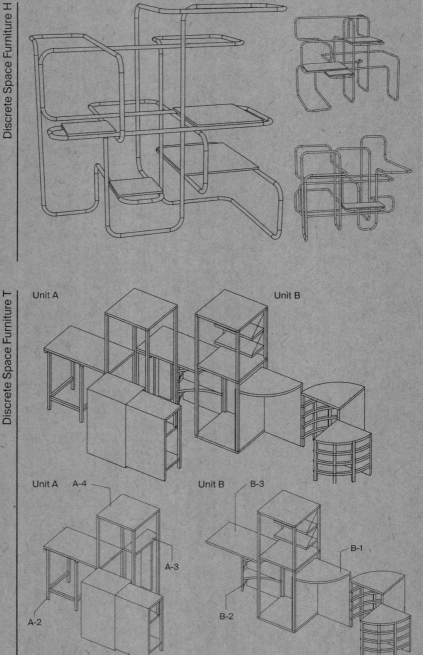

Discrete Space Furniture H

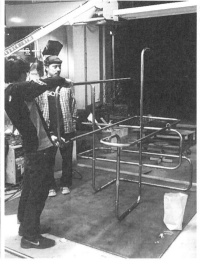

Discrete Space Furniture T

● Study of "Discrete Space Furniture." It will be used for marches held at public spaces in new towns.

● ニュータウンの公共空間でマルシェを開催するための家具「離散空間家具」のスタディ

444 | 10.0 | Postscript

Postscript

10.0

10.0 | あとがき

I realized that architecture involves not only "knowledge of forms" but also the act of "giving a form to knowledge" when I was designing Shop U in 2005. Even though I had no experience of designing a tableware store at that time, it was a joyful endeavor to transform our idea into a form step by step while learning about the tableware store from our client. The outcome turned out to be a form that neither I nor the client expected. The experience of giving a form to something we had had no knowledge of into and then gain new knowledge from a "form we hadn't known" was full of discoveries.
—

A "form" is not only something one sees in a single model. It is difficult to understand the meaning of a single model by seeing it alone. But you begin to see its meaning when you compare it with another model. In this sense, the difference between the two models is the key to understanding their "forms." After a project proceeds to a certain degree, we are able to see models as a group and understand their "forms" by objectively observing the sequential development from the first to the latest models. The "form of knowledge" evolves through mutual feedbacks between a "group of forms reflecting knowledge" and "knowledge learned from a group of forms developed in time sequence."
—

We only need to follow a few rules in the procedure of making "a group of forms developed in time sequence": models and drawings should be made at the same scale and laid out in time sequence so that they can be compared easily. While it requires significant energy to keep repeating the simple procedure, an archive of results gained through continued efforts eventually formulates a set of reliable references.
—

It is also important to set certain rules in order to prevent degrading the simple procedure to mere "routine work." In designing BUILDING K, we made a rule to "come up with two schemes every week" to keep up the pace. When we designed "Facility for Ecology Education" in 2012, we made a rule to "hold a two-hour meeting every two weeks and repeat it five times" and spent great amount of energy in keeping a good rhythm in the studio.
—

While it is important to maintain a "linear" state where an

建築とは「かたちについての知識」であると同時に「知識をかたちにすること」だと実感したのは、2005年に「Shop U」を設計していたときのことだ。当時、食器を販売する店舗を設計したことはなかったが、クライアントからお店のことについて教えてもらいながら、ちょっとずつかたちにする作業が楽しかった。最終形は私もクライアントも想像していなかったかたちをしていた。知らなかったことをかたちにして、出来上がった「知らなかったかたち」からまた新しいことを学ぶ、という経験は、とても発見的だった。

—

ひとつの模型からみえるものだけが「かたち」ではない。模型はそれひとつではその意味するところがよくわからない。だがふたつの模型を比較すると、その模型の意味がみえてくる。そう考えると、ふたつの模型の差分が「かたち」を読み取る鍵になる。そしてプロジェクトがある程度進んでくると、今後は模型を「群として」みることが可能になり、始まりから現在までの進化を俯瞰的にみることで把握できる「かたち」もある。「ちのかたち」は「知識の反映としてのかたちの群れ」と「時系列を伴ったかたちの群れから学ぶ知識」が相互にフィードバックすることで進化していく。

—

「時系列を伴ったかたちの群れ」をつくるために気をつけることはわずかなことだ。模型や図面をつくるとき、それらを同じ縮尺でつくる、時系列に並べるなど、比較を可能にするわずかな工夫を続けることである。単純作業を維持するのにはエネルギーを要するが、継続すると作業の総体が参照可能なアーカイヴとして力をもってくる。

—

単純作業が形骸化に回収されないようにするための工夫も必要だろう。「BUILDING K」の設計に際しては「毎週ふたつの案をつくる」と決めて、リズムをキープすることに集中していた。2012年の「鶴ヶ島プロジェクト」も「2週間に1回2時間のミーティングを5回反復する」というルールを定め、スタジオのなかでリズムを維持することにエネルギーを費やした。

—

時間と成果が正比例となる「線形」的な状態を維持するのも重要なことだが（世の中には時間と成果が比例しないことのほうが多い）、時間とともに成果がべき乗に比例するように向上する状況を「超線形」と名付け、目標としてきた。その違いが「工学主義」と「批判的工学主義」の違いをつくるからだ。クリエイティビティを、インスピレーションのような偶然性に期待するのとは異なり、再現性を重視するという意味では工学的であることが重要だが、それが形骸化を避け、創造性を高め

accomplishment and time are directly proportional to each other (although that is seldom the case in the real world), we have aimed to create a "super linear" state where an accomplishment is exponentially proportional to time. The difference between the "linear" and "super linear" distinguishes "Critical Engineering-ism" from "Engineering-ism."

—

It is important to take an engineering approach in our efforts to achieve creativity out of logical necessity without depending on sheer chance or inspiration. In order to enhance creativity while avoiding falling into routine work, we need to clarify and implement an effective process for generating the "form of knowledge."

—

This book is an archive of our trials and errors in search of the "form of knowledge", which we also expect to serve as a new resource in the further pursuit of the "form of knowledge." This book gave us an opportunity to look back at a series of architecture we built and review them as a group of forms developed in time sequence. In my view, our next challenge is to develop our architectural vocabulary further. Our design up to today was based on a conventional architectural vocabulary including a pitched roof and aluminum window sash. From now on, we would like to focus on developing a new vocabulary by utilizing machine languages, and this direction is already evident in some of our works presented in this book.

—

These projects exploring the "form of knowledge" couldn't have been realized without generous support from all those involved. Our deepest gratitude goes first to our clients for giving us the wonderful opportunities, as well as former and current staff at RFA, my students and assistants for their tremendous efforts and support through it all. We sincerely thank Kumiko Ikada, Mitsuaki Hashida, Mariko Katagiri and everyone at TOTO Gallery Ma for organizing the exhibition "The Form of Knowledge"; Sakae Shimizu, Hiroyo Furukawa and everyone at TOTO Publishing as well as translator Kazuko Sakamoto for their great work and support in publishing this book. I am also grateful to Yuzo Kariya and Nao Kakuta for their appealing editorial design and Yoshikazu Nango for his brilliant commentary.

るためにも「ちのかたち」の生成プロセスがクリアになっていることが有効に働く。

本書の刊行はこれまでの「ちのかたち」をめぐる試行錯誤のアーカイブであると同時に、新たな「ちのかたち」の試行錯誤の新たな参照源となるだろう。本書を通じて自分の実現してきた建築を改めて「時系列を伴ったかたちの群れ」としてもういちど眺め直してみると、語彙の開発が課題であると感じる。これまでは勾配屋根やアルミサッシの引き違い窓など、慣習的な語彙をもとに設計してきたが、今後は最後に萌芽的に示したように、機械言語も駆使した新しい語彙の創出に力を入れていきたい。

「ちのかたち」をめぐる試行錯誤は、周囲の方々の支えなしにはなし得なかった。クライアントをはじめ、試行錯誤をともにしたRFAの歴代スタッフや学生諸氏、アシスタントの皆さんには感謝したい。そして「ちのかたち」と題した展示の実現にあたっては筏久美子氏、橋田光明氏、片桐真理子氏をはじめとするTOTOギャラリー・間の皆様、本書の刊行にあたっては清水栄江氏、古川浩代氏をはじめとするTOTO出版の皆様、翻訳をしてくださった坂本和子氏に大変お世話になった。また刈谷悠三氏、角田奈央氏の魅力的なエディトリアルデザインと、南後由和氏の素晴らしい解説には舌を巻いた。記して感謝申し上げたい。

11.0 | Data

450

11.0

Data

| 11.0 | データ

Data on Works

—

—

•	Project title	
	Number	Page
1	Location	
2	Completion date	
3	Design period	
4	Construction period	
5	Building type	
6	Collaboration	
7	Structure	
8	Number of stories	
9	Structural engineer	
10	Building services engineer	
11	Other design	
12	Construction	
13	Site area	
14	Building area	
15	Total floor area	

• Odaka Pioneer Village

	0.3	p.034
1	Minamisoma, Fukushima, Japan	
2	2018.9	
3	2017.2-2018.1	
4	2018.2-2018.6	
5	Meeting Place, guest house, co-working office	
7	Steel frame	
8	2 stories	
9	Structural Design: Mitsuhiro Kanada/Tokyo University of the Arts	
	Structural Engineer: TECTONICA	
10	Kankyo Engineering	
11	Lighting: tuki lighting office	
12	Trust One	
13	415.43m²	
14	156.26m²	
15	280.08m²	

• SHOP U

	1.1	p.056
1	Saitama, Japan	
2	2005.12	
3	2005.7-2005.11	
4	2005.11-2005.12	
5	Retail	
12	Yumita Builder	
14	31.6m²	

• BUILDING K

	1.2	p.072
1	Suginami, Tokyo, Japan	
2	2008.5	
3	2005.8-2007.5	
4	2007.6-2008.5	
5	Apartment + Retail	
7	Steel frame	
8	6 stories	
9	Ohno-Japan	
10	Kankyo Engineering	
12	Maruzen kensetsu kogyo	
13	559.38m²	
14	346.02m²	
15	1,611.37m²	

• Building HOUSE

	2.1	p.098
1	Kanagawa, Japan	
2	2009.3	
3	2007.12-2008.9	
4	2008.10-2009.3	
5	House	
7	Wood frame	
8	3 stories	
9	Ohno-Japan	
12	Daisyo Construction	
13	65.39m²	
14	32.77m²	
15	96.83m²	

• Storage HOUSE

	2.2	p.112
1	Kanagawa, Japan	
2	2011.4	
3	2009.8-2010.9	
4	2010.10-2011.4	
5	House	
7	Steel frame + reinforced concrete	
8	1 basement, 2 stories	
9	Konishi Structural Engineers	
12	Shinoki Koumuten	
13	57.82m²	
14	31.60m²	
15	56.26m²	

• Shed HOUSE

	2.3	p.132
1	Kanagawa, Japan	
2	2011.10	
3	2009.9-2010.11	
4	2010.12-2011.10	
5	House	
7	Wood frame + reinforced concrete	
8	2 stories	
9	Ohno-Japan	
12	HEISEI Corporation	
13	156.12m²	
14	61.54m²	
15	97.06m²	

• House HOUSE

	2.4	p.146
1	Tokyo, Japan	
2	2012.11	
3	2011.3-2012.4	
4	2012.4-2012.11	
5	House	
7	Wood frame	
8	2 stories	
9	Kinoshita Structural Engineers	
12	Taishin Kensetsu	
13	108.01m²	
14	48.90m²	
15	84.27m²	

• Facility for Ecology Education

	3.2	p.182
1	Tsurugashima, Saitama, Japan	
2	2014.3	
3	2013.4-2013.8	
4	2013.9-2014.2	
5	Facility for Ecology Education	
6	Ryuji Fujimura + Kazumi Kudo / Toyo University Social Design Studio	
7	Wood frame	
8	1 story	
9	Jun Sato Structural Engineers	
10	Sato Facility Engineer	
11	Lighting: tuki lighting office	
	Furniture: neu furniture works	
	Curtain: Yoko Ando Design	
	Sign: neucitora	
12	Yanagawa Koumuten	
13	499.00m²	
14	127.82m²	
15	127.82m²	

• Aichi Project

	4.1	p.208
1	Aichi Triennale 2013	
2	2013.8	
3	2013.8.10-2013.10.27	

• G Chair

	4.2	p.224
1	Materializing [II]	
2	2014.7	
5	Chair	

• G House

	4.3	p.234
1	MAKEHOUSE	
2	2014.10	
3	2014.6-2014.10	

作品データ
—
●

● 作品名
　ナンバー　　　　　　ページ
1 所在地
2 竣工年月
3 設計期間
4 施工期間
5 主要用途
6 共同設計
7 構造
8 規模
9 構造設計
10 設備設計
11 その他設計
12 施工
13 敷地面積
14 建築面積
15 延床面積

● 小高パイオニアビレッジ
　0.3　　　　　　p.034
1 福島県南相馬市
2 2018.9
3 2017.2-2018.1
4 2018.2-2018.6
5 集会所、事務所、簡易宿所
7 鉄骨造
8 地上2階
9 構造計画：
　金田充弘／東京藝術大学
　構造設計：TECTONICA
10 環境エンジニアリング
11 照明：ツキライティングオフィス
12 トラストワン
13 415.43m²
14 156.26m²
15 280.08m²

● SHOP U
　1.1　　　　　　p.056
1 埼玉県和光市
2 2005.12
3 2005.7-2005.11
4 2005.11-2005.12
5 店舗
12 弓田工務店
14 31.6m²

● BUILDING K
　1.2　　　　　　p.072
1 東京都杉並区
2 2008.5
3 2005.8-2007.5
4 2007.6-2008.5
5 共同住宅、店舗

7 鉄骨造
8 地上6階
9 オーノJAPAN
10 環境エンジニアリング
12 丸善建設工業
13 559.38m²
14 346.02m²
15 1,611.37m²

● ビルの家
　2.1　　　　　　p.098
1 神奈川県川崎市
2 2009.3
3 2007.12-2008.9
4 2008.10-2009.3
5 住宅
7 木造
8 地上3階
9 オーノJAPAN
12 大勝建設
13 65.39m²
14 32.77m²
15 96.83m²

● 倉庫の家
　2.2　　　　　　p.112
1 神奈川県
2 2011.4
3 2009.8-2010.9
4 2010.10-2011.4
5 住宅
7 鉄骨造＋RC造
8 地下1階、地上2階
9 小西泰孝建築構造設計
12 篠木工務店
13 57.82m²
14 31.60m²
15 56.26m²

● 小屋の家
　2.3　　　　　　p.132
1 神奈川県横須賀市
2 2011.10
3 2009.9-2010.11
4 2010.12-2011.10
5 住宅
7 木造＋RC造
8 地上2階
9 オーノJAPAN
12 平成建設
13 156.12m²
14 61.54m²
15 97.06m²

● 家の家
　2.4　　　　　　p.146
1 東京都
2 2012.11
3 2011.3-2012.4

4 2012.4-2012.11
5 住宅
7 木造
8 地上2階
9 木下洋介構造計画
12 泰進建設
13 108.01m²
14 48.90m²
15 84.27m²

● 鶴ヶ島太陽光発電所
　環境教育施設
　3.2　　　　　　p.182
1 埼玉県鶴ヶ島市
2 2014.3
3 2013.4-2013.8
4 2013.9-2014.2
5 環境教育施設
6 藤村龍至＋工藤和美／
　東洋大学ソーシャル
　デザインスタジオ
7 木造
8 地上1階
9 佐藤淳構造設計事務所
10 佐藤設備設計
11 照明：ツキライティングオフィス
　家具：ニュウファニチャー
　ワークス
　カーテン：安東陽子デザイン
　サイン：neucitora
12 柳川工務店
13 499.00m²
14 127.82m²
15 127.82m²

● あいちプロジェクト
　4.1　　　　　　p.208
1 あいちトリエンナーレ2013
2 2013.8
3 2013.8.10-2013.10.27

● G Chair
　4.2　　　　　　p.224
1 マテリアライジング展Ⅱ
2 2014.7
5 椅子

● G House
　4.3　　　　　　p.234
1 MAKEHOUSE
2 2014.10
3 2014.6-2014.10
5 住宅
6 NCN

● 白岡ニュータウン
　プロジェクト
　4.4　　　　　　p.242
1 埼玉県白岡市

5	House	
6	NCN	

• Shiraoka Newtown Project

	4.4	p.242
1	Shiraoka, Saitama, Japan	
2	2016.4	
3	2015.2-2015.8	
4	2015.8-2016.4	
5	House	
7	Wood Frame + Safety Engineering	
8	2 stories	
9	NCN	
11	Exterior: Hajime Ishikawa Lighting: tuki lighting office	
12	Itohpia Home	
13	9-7(A): 246.75m² 9-6(B): 170.06m² 9-5(C): 201.80m² 9-4(D): 183.62m² 9-3(E): 202.17m²	
14	9-7(A): 74.25m² 9-6(B): 53.00m² 9-5(C): 74.25m² 9-4(D): 64.53m² 9-3(E): 74.25m²	
15	9-7(A): 120.19m² 9-6(B): 85.39m² 9-5(C): 129.28m² 9-4(D): 110.76m² 9-3(E): 131.77m²	

• APARTMENT S

	5.1	p.264
1	Meguro, Tokyo, Japan	
2	2011.2	
3	2009.7-2010.5	
4	2010.6-2011.2	
5	Apartment	
7	Reinforced concrete	
8	5 stories	
9	Konishi Structural Engineers	
12	Hayashida Architects	
13	102.80m²	
14	60.93m²	
15	302.23m²	

• APARTMENT B

	5.2	p.276
1	Meguro, Tokyo, Japan	
2	2013.3	
3	2010.11-2012.6	
4	2012.7-2013.3	
5	Apartment	
7	Reinforced concrete	
8	3 stories	
9	Konishi Structural Engineers	

12	Hayashida Architects	
13	99.18m²	
14	68.04m²	
15	182.18m²	

• APARTMENT N

	5.3	p.288
1	Meguro, Tokyo, Japan	
2	2014.6	
3	2013.1-2013.9	
4	2013.10-2014.6	
5	Apartment	
7	Reinforced concrete	
8	3 stories	
9	Konishi Structural Engineers	
12	Hayashida Architects	
13	70.16m²	
14	36.30m²	
15	122.52m²	

• OM TERRACE

	6.1	p.310
1	Saitama, Japan	
2	2017.4	
3	2016.4-2016.10	
4	2016.12-2017.4	
5	Community Cycle Port, Public Toilet	
7	Steel frame	
8	1 story with a penthouse	
9	Konishi Structural Engineers	
10	Kankyo Engineering	
11	Lighting: tuki lighting office Building Estimation: Acost Sign: neucitora	
12	Yamazaki Koumuten	
13	240.61m²	
14	173.00m²	
15	179.25m²	

• Tsurugashima CentralCommunity Center

	6.2	p.334
1	Tsurugashima, Saitama, Japan	
2	2018.3	
3	2017.4-2017.8	
4	2017.9-2018.3	
5	Meeting place	
7	Steel frame	
8	1 story	
9	Structural Design: Mitsuhiro Kanada/Tokyo University of the Arts Strucutural Engineer: TECTONICA	
10	Kankyo Engineering	

11	Lighting: tuki lighting office Building Estimation: Acost Sign: neucitora	
12	Toyo Construction	
13	977.01m²	
14	326.00m²	
15	321.34m²	

• Subaru Nursery School

	7.1	p.358
1	Ogori, Fukuoka, Japan	
2	2018.3	
3	2016.8-2017.8	
4	2017.9-2018.3	
5	Nursery school	
6	Ryuji Fujimura/RFA + Hayashida Shunji/CFA	
7	Reinforced concrete	
8	1 story	
9	Mitsuda Structural Consultants	
10	Sintoshi Setsubi-Sekkei	
11	Lighting: tuki lighting office Curtain: Yoko Ando Design Sign: neucitora ZEB Planner: Tateyoshi	
12	Tateyoshi	
13	5,718.42m²	
14	1,281.88m²	
15	1,203.43m²	

• Deep Learning Chair

	7.2	p.392
1	Ryuji Fujimura: The Form of Knowledge	
2	2018.7	
3	2018.1-2018.7	
5	Chair	
6	Programming: Junichiro Horikawa	

• Study of "Discrete Space"

	9.0	p.429
1	Ryuji Fujimura: The Form of Knowledge	
2	2018.7	
3	2017.7-2018.7	
6	Ryuji Fujimura Laboratory, Tokyo University of the Arts	
11	Graphic design: neucitora	

2　2016.4
3　2015.2-2015.8
4　2015.8-2016.4
5　住宅
7　木造＋SE構法
8　地上2階
9　エヌ・シー・エヌ
11　外構：石川初
　　照明：ツキライティングオフィス
12　イトーピアホーム
13　9-7(A): 246.75m²
　　9-6(B): 170.06m²
　　9-5(C): 201.80m²
　　9-4(D): 183.62m²
　　9-3(E): 202.17m²
14　9-7(A): 74.25m²
　　9-6(B): 53.00m²
　　9-5(C): 74.25m²
　　9-4(D): 64.53m²
　　9-3(E): 74.25m²
15　9-7(A): 120.19m²
　　9-6(B): 85.39m²
　　9-5(C): 129.28m²
　　9-4(D): 110.76m²
　　9-3(E): 131.77m²

• APARTMENT S
　　5.1　　　　p.264
1　東京都目黒区
2　2011.2
3　2009.7-2010.5
4　2010.6-2011.2
5　共同住宅
7　RC造
8　地上5階
9　小西泰孝建築構造設計
12　林田建設
13　102.80m²
14　60.93m²
15　302.23m²

• APARTMENT B
　　5.2　　　　p.276
1　東京都目黒区
2　2013.3
3　2010.11-2012.6
4　2012.7-2013.3
5　共同住宅
7　RC造
8　地上3階
9　小西泰孝建築構造設計
12　林田建設
13　99.18m²
14　68.04m²
15　182.18m²

• APARTMENT N
　　5.3　　　　p.288
1　東京都目黒区

2　2014.6
3　2013.1-2013.9
4　2013.10-2014.6
5　共同住宅
7　RC造
8　地上3階
9　小西泰孝建築構造設計
12　林田建設
13　70.16m²
14　36.30m²
15　122.52m²

• OM TERRACE
　　6.1　　　　p.310
1　埼玉県さいたま市
2　2017.4
3　2016.4-2016.10
4　2016.12-2017.4
5　コミュニティサイクルポート、
　　公衆便所
7　鉄骨造
8　地上1階、塔屋1階
9　小西泰孝建築構造設計
10　環境エンジニアリング
11　照明：ツキライティングオフィス
　　積算：アコスト
　　サイン：neucitora
12　山崎工務店
13　240.61m²
14　173.00m²
15　179.25m²

• つるがしま 中央交流センター
　　6.2　　　　p.334
1　埼玉県鶴ヶ島市
2　2018.3
3　2017.4-2017.8
4　2017.9-2018.3
5　集会所
7　鉄骨造
8　地上1階
9　構造計画：
　　金田充弘／東京藝術大学
　　構造設計：TECTONICA
10　環境エンジニアリング
11　照明：ツキライティングオフィス
　　積算：アコスト
　　サイン：neucitora
12　東洋建設
13　977.01m²
14　326.00m²
15　321.34m²

• すばる保育園
　　7.1　　　　p.358
1　福岡県小郡市
2　2018.3
3　2016.8-2017.8

4　2017.9-2018.3
5　保育園
6　藤村龍至／RFA＋
　　林田俊二／CFA
7　RC造
8　地上1階
9　満田衛資構造計画研究所
10　新都市設備設計
11　照明：ツキライティングオフィス
　　カーテン：安東陽子デザイン
　　サイン：neucitora
　　ZEBプランナー：建吉組
12　太陽建設工業
13　5,718.42m²
14　1,281.88m²
15　1,203.43m²

• Deep Learning Chair
　　7.2　　　　p.392
1　ちのかたち 藤村龍至展
2　2018.7
3　2018.1-2018.7
4　椅子
6　プログラミング：堀川淳一郎

• 「離散空間」のスタディ
　　9.0　　　　p.429
1　ちのかたち 藤村龍至展
2　2018.7
3　2017.7-2018.7
6　東京藝術大学 藤村研究室
11　グラフィックデザイン：
　　neucitora

Profile

Ryuji Fujimura

1976	Born in Tokyo, Japan.
2005-	Established Ryuji Fujimura Architects (RFA).
2008	Withdrew from the doctoral program at the Graduate School of Architecture, Tokyo Institute of Technology, upon earing all required credits
2010-2016	Lecturer at Toyo University.
2016-	Associate professor at Tokyo University of the Arts.

略歴

藤村龍至

1976	東京生まれ
2005-	藤村龍至建築設計事務所（現RFA）主宰
2008	東京工業大学大学院博士課程単位取得退学
2010-2016	東洋大学専任講師
2016-	東京藝術大学准教授

photo: Gottingham

Staff List

Current Staff Members

Makiko Fujimura
Yuko Kitayama
Daisuke Takechi
Yoshikazu Sato
Ukei Fukuda
Kei Takahashi
Tomoka Suganuma
Renri Yamamoto
Yurika Mantoku

Formor Staff Members

Kazuho Ogasawara
Kazuya Kitayama
Keisuke Ito
Satoshi Numanui
Katsutoshi Hata
Yuichi Nishimura
Yu Sakurai
Tamotsu Ito
Makoto Shiroma

スタッフリスト

現スタッフ

藤村眞樹子
北山裕子
武智大祐
佐藤芳和
福田宇啓
高橋慧
菅沼朋香
山本蓮理
万徳友里香

旧スタッフ

小笠原一穂
高野和哉
伊藤啓輔
沼野井諭
畑克敏
西村祐一
櫻井佑
伊藤維
城間真琴

Credits | クレジット

Photographs | 写真

- RFA | unless otherwise specified | 記載ない限り
- Takumi Ota | 太田拓実 | pp.112-113, p.115, pp.118-119, p.121, p.123, p.125, p.127, pp129-133, p.135, pp.138-139, p.141, pp.143-147, p.149, p.153, pp.155-163, pp.165-166, p.183, pp.192-193, p.201(上), pp.204-205, p.259, pp.264-265, p.267, p.271, pp.273-277, p.279, pp.282-283, pp.285-289, p.291, p.295, pp.297-303, pp.310-313, p.315, p.321, p.323, pp.325-327, pp.329-330, pp.332-335, p.337, pp.342-345, p.347-355, pp.358-359, pp.361-363, pp.368-375, pp.378-383, pp.390-391
- Yoshihiro Kikuyama | 菊山義浩 | pp.208-209, p.212, p.214(左上)
- Gottingham | pp.005-009, pp.260-261, pp.306-307, p.456
- Kenshu Shintsubo | 新津保建秀 | pp.016-017, pp.020-023, pp.028-035, pp.048-050, p.053, pp.416-417
- Fujimura Laboratory, Tokyo University of the Arts | 東京藝術大学藤村研究室 | p.429, pp.436-443
- Dep. of Architecture, Toyo University | 東洋大学建築学科 | p.171, pp.174-176, p.177(上段4枚), p.184, p.187, p.189, pp.194-195, p.197, pp.202-203
- Koichi Torimura | 鳥村鋼一 | p.059, pp.062-063, pp.065-067, pp.072-073, p.075, p.083(下), p.085(下), p.087(下), pp.090-095
- Anna Nagai | 永井杏奈 | pp.242-245, p.247, pp.254-255, p.257-258
- Javiel Callejas Sevilla | ハビエル・カレハス・セビリア | pp.080-081, p.083(上,中), p.085(上,中), p.087(上)
- Kenichi Higuchi | 樋口兼一 | pp.098-101, pp.105-107, pp.109-111
- Koji Fujimura and Norihiko Okada | p.078
- hiyang.on.flickr | p.317(右)

Figure | 図版

- Mitsuda Structural Consultants | 満田衛資構造計画研究所 | p.384, pp.388-389

Image Source | 出典

- p.003 | Author: Christopher Alexander, *Notes on the Synthesis of Form*, Harvard University Press., 1964 || p.003 | クリストファー・アレグザンダー著『形の合成に関するノート』(1964)
- pp.016-017, pp.020-021 | Ed. Hiroki Azuma, TOURIZING FUKUSHIMA: THE FUKUICHI KANKO PROJECT (genron, 2013) || pp.016-017, pp.020-021 | 東浩紀編著『福島第一原発観光地化計画 思想地図beta vol.4-2』(ゲンロン, 2013)
- p.027 | *shisouchizu beta* vol.2 (Contectures, 2011) || p.027 | 『思想地図beta vol.2』(コンテクチュアズ, 2011)
- p.177(bottom, middle) | Yomiuri Shinbun, 22 October 2012 p.15, Tokyo, Japan: The Yomiuri Shinbun. || p.177(下段:中)| 『読売新聞』2012年10月22日 朝刊 15面
- p.177(bottom, top left second photo) | Asahi Shinbun, 12 December 2012, p.38, Tokyo, Japan: The Asahi Shinbun. || p.177(下段:左上2枚目)| 『朝日新聞』2012年12月12日 朝刊 38面
- p.177(bottom, top left first photo) | Asahi Shinbun, 6 August 2013, p.28. || p.177(下段:左上1枚目)| 『朝日新聞』2013年8月6日 朝刊 28面
- p.177(bottom, right) | Asahi Shinbun, 19 November 2013, p.17. || p.177(下段:右)| 『朝日新聞』2013年11月19日 朝刊 17面
- p.177(bottom, bottom left) | The Nihon Keizai Shinbun, 18 February 2014, p.9, Tokyo, Japan: Nikkei, Inc. || p.177(下段:左下)| 『日本経済新聞』2014年2月18日 夕刊 9面
- p.317(left/左) | El Croquis 131-132: OMA + Rem Koolhaas 1996-2007: vol.I

Collaborator in drawings: Mari Takahashi | 図面協力：髙橋まり

English Translations: Kazuko Sakamoto | 英文翻訳：坂本和子

English Proofreading: Harutaka Oribe | 英文校閲：織部晴崇

The Form of Knowledge-
The Prototype of Architectural Thinking
and Its Application
—
First published in Japan on August 21, 2018
Second published on September 25, 2020
—
[Author]
Ryuji Fujimura
—
[Publisher]
Takeshi Ito
—
TOTO Publishing (TOTO LTD.)
TOTO Nogizaka Bldg., 2F
1-24-3 Minami-Aoyama, Minato-ku
Tokyo 107-0062, Japan
Sales | Telephone: +81-3-3402-7138
Facsimile: +81-3-3402-7187
Editorial | Telephone: +81-3-3497-1010
URL: https://jp.toto.com/publishing
—
[Designer]
Yuzo Kariya + Nao Kakuta / neucitora
[Design Cooperation]
Yoshikazu Sato / RFA
—
[Printer]
Tosho Printing Co., LTD.
—
—
Except as permitted under copyright law, this
book may not be reproduced, in whole or in
part, in any form or by any means, including
photocopying, scanning, digitizing, or otherwise,
without prior permission. Scanning or digitizing
this book through a third party, even for personal
or home use, is also strictly prohibited.
The list price is indicated on the cover.
—
© 2018 Ryuji Fujimura
—
—
Printed in Japan
ISBN978-4-88706-374-7

ちのかたち——
建築的思考のプロトタイプとその応用
—
2018年8月21日 第1刷発行
2020年9月25日 第2刷発行
—
[著者]
藤村龍至
—
[発行者]
伊藤剛士
—
[発行所]
TOTO出版（TOTO株式会社）
〒107-0062 東京都港区南青山1-24-3
TOTO乃木坂ビル2F
営業 | TEL: 03-3402-7138 | FAX: 03-3402-7187
編集 | TEL: 03-3497-1010
URL: https://jp.toto.com/publishing
—
[デザイン]
刈谷悠三＋角田奈央／neucitora
[デザイン協力]
佐藤芳和／RFA
—
[印刷・製本]
図書印刷株式会社
—
落丁本・乱丁本はお取り替えいたします。
本書の全部又は一部に対する
コピー・スキャン・デジタル化等の無断複製行為は、
著作権法上での例外を除き禁じます。
本書を代行業者等の第三者に依頼して
スキャンやデジタル化することは、
たとえ個人や家庭内での利用であっても
著作権上認められておりません。
定価はカバーに表示してあります。
—
© 2018 Ryuji Fujimura
—
—
Printed in Japan
ISBN978-4-88706-374-7